$\mathcal{E}$xotics
ARE EASY

Wiltshire College
Lackham

Lacock
Chippenham
Wiltshire
SN15 2NY   Tel: 01249 466814

Exotics

ARE EASY

GUILD OF MASTER CRAFTSMAN PUBLICATIONS LTD

This collection first published 2001 by
Guild of Master Craftsman Publications Ltd,
166 High Street, Lewes,
East Sussex BN7 1XU

© GMC Publications 2001

Reprinted 2002

ISBN 1 86108 231 2

Front cover photographs: (main picture) Mark Baker, (inset, top to bottom)
Myles Challis, Harry Smith Photographic Collection, Shirley-Anne Bell

Back cover photographs: (background) Harry Smith Photographic Collection, (inset, top to
bottom) John Williamson, Chris Skarbon, Harry Smith Photographic Collection, Shirley-Anne Bell,
Thompson & Morgan Seed Company, Harry Smith Photographic Collection

Article photography by kind permission of the contributors, GMC Photographic Studio and
Harry Smith Photographic Collection, with the exception of the following: Tony King (p18-19),
Kobakoba (p74, top left, p76), Lyn Spencer-Mills (p74-75), The Palm Centre (p94),
Mike Pilcher (p107)

Many thanks to Cathy Elliott for lending her Mac and design skills
to the production of this book.

Printed and bound by Kyodo Printing (Singapore) under the supervision of
MRM Graphics, Winslow, Buckinghamshire, UK

CONTENTS

INTRODUCTION

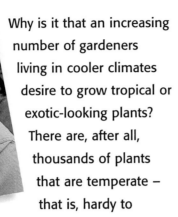

Why is it that an increasing number of gardeners living in cooler climates desire to grow tropical or exotic-looking plants? There are, after all, thousands of plants that are temperate – that is, hardy to freezing point and effectively a little below – but which look as though they have come straight off a desert island or from the jungle deep! I am positive that the recent popularity of such plants is partly because they remind us of holidays abroad – the Mediterranean, the Caribbean, Australia, China, and so on. For some, the size, boldness and 'architectural' nature of the plants means that they make a statement in the garden. And some of us, of course, grow exotic plants because they are just a bit... different!

In the spring of 2000 a magazine was launched in the UK, dedicated to the growing of hardy exotics. *Exotic & Greenhouse Gardening* immediately became a winner, and I can honestly say that of the various gardening magazines I have had the pleasure to edit over the past two decades, it is this magazine that has given me most pleasure. The readers, all of them keen to learn about and grow more of these plants, are passionate people. They have been extremely vociferous in their demands on the magazine: what they want in it, and what they want to learn from it. They want to see some excellent pictures, too!

This book is a compilation of some of the best features from the first year of the magazine's life. Here you will see contributions from some of the most knowledgeable people from the world of exotic gardening. First, there is Myles Challis (the foremost 'exoticist' who effectively created the genre), Martin Gibbons (the man who knows more about palms than anyone else), Shirley-Anne Bell (a leading grower of cactus and succulent plants), Christopher Holliday (who maintains the National Collection of Phormiums), Freda Cox (Chairman of the UK branch of the Mediterranean Garden Society), and so on.

What do you need in order to become a fully fledged 'exoticist'? Well, you don't have to be rich. You don't have to have a five-acre garden. You don't even have to be an expert gardener. All you really need is a love of plants and a desire to try something different. Armed with these, you'll be able to create your own exotic paradise. Go on, have a go.

Happy gardening!

Graham Clarke

Graham Clarke
Editor
Exotic & Greenhouse Gardening magazine

Setting the scene for Seduction

Exotic gardens designer Myles Challis, who has done more than anyone else to popularise the genre, writes about this all-consuming passion for 'exoticism'

TOP: Exotic plantings can look even more authentic in early morning mist, or when light diffuses between the lush growth

LEFT: Myles Challis – at home when surrounded by leafy exotics

If you have been buying and planting palms, bamboos, bananas and the like, then whether you realise it or not, you are now what is generally referred to as an 'exoticist'.

My own exotic garden at home in East London had generated considerable interest, and it was suggested that I should design for others, and eventually exhibit at the Chelsea Flower Show.

The first show garden, in 1986, was met with a certain amount of bewilderment. One lady thought that the displays were made from house plants – understandable to a degree, considering that nobody had seen bananas growing with hostas before.

Little did I realise then that it was to trigger the start of an entirely new trend in gardening.

At the time there were no specialist nurseries so many of the plants were difficult to obtain, but following the show I was quickly contacted by nurserymen for information.

Plant exchanges took place with gardeners in places like Cornwall, and even botanical gardens, and soon nurseries like Architectural Plants and Hardy Exotics appeared, making it easier to buy the plants and generally raising the profile of exotic gardening.

Soon after this I was asked to write a book, *The Exotic Garden*, and the ball had started rolling!

The Victorians
Though my Chelsea garden was apparently the first of its kind, I cannot claim credit for the introduction of exotic gardening to the UK. The Victorians originally conceived

it and referred to it as 'subtropical' or 'wild' gardening.

Their method was very labour-intensive, which was fine at a time when labour – and fuel – was cheap. It consisted chiefly of moving the contents of large greenhouses outside for the summer months to create 'picturesque' effects.

The flaw with this was that most plants were truly tropical and, though they survived, they made little perceivable growth.

After the demise of the Victorian methods, due in the main to the wars and increased costs for labour and fuel, exotic gardening was mainly confined to our gulf stream gardens, like those in Cornwall and at Tresco in the Isles of Scilly, where the mild climate has always permitted the growing of more tender plants.

What I did 20 years ago was to reintroduce the subject in a way

more suited to modern lifestyles. I use mostly hardy but exotic-looking plants such as palms, bamboos, cordylines, phormiums, tree-ferns, and so on, permanently planted outside with a few tender plants such as cannas, gingers and daturas (brugmansias) to provide summer colour. It is altogether a more practical and less costly scenario.

Three great qualities
Though slow initially, exoticism has really taken off in the past few years and now hardly a week passes by without bold and exotic plants appearing on TV gardening programmes – no great surprise when you consider that exoticism has three great qualities:

i) the 'instant' effect – most exotic plants have a fast rate of growth which makes it possible to create established-looking gardens, either immediately or

The Abyssinian banana

Henry Cooke - the pioneer

There was one pioneer of exotics to whom I shall always owe a debt of gratitude.

In the early 1980s, when I was in the early stages of discovering plants, I was eager to locate even more lush and tropical-looking subjects. So I spent ages searching through old books, looking for plants to create the desired effects.

One day I picked up a little book written 100 years ago, called *A Gloucestershire Wild Garden*, written anonymously by someone calling himself the 'Curator'. It fell open at an amazing black-and-white photograph of a glade in the author's garden.

In a group of assorted exotics were two Abyssinian bananas (*Ensete ventricosum*) that must have been 6m (20ft) high. I realised straight away that I could achieve my aspirations.

The author of the book had served as surgeon-general in the army in India and had been so taken by the gardens he saw during his spell there that he determined on his return to try to recreate one.

He had to search for many months to find his ideal site – a south-west facing area surrounded with woodland in a U-shaped valley, in the Forest of Dean, Gloucestershire.

His achievements were considerable. He built large greenhouses to accommodate his tender plants, including his Abyssinian bananas.

These were planted out each summer and had to be taken up each autumn and moved inside; local farm labourers and a team of horses were employed to drag the plants the several hundred yards each time.

On discovering the author's name (Henry Cooke) I decided to try and find the location of the garden in case any remnant of it had survived. The best part of a century had passed, so I held out little hope.

Eventually I located both the site and its present owners, who had already discovered its history. I was invited down, though I was warned that I might be disappointed. I arrived on a summer's day and was greeted warmly by the owners who had started trying to restore the garden.

Little had remained of the original plantings, bar two Chusan palms, a few bamboos and forests of a rampaging knotweed (polygonum), which no doubt had been responsible for the demise of many of the plants.

There is one final part to this story. In 1985 a film was made on the site. Called *The Assam Garden*, it starred Deborah Kerr as a widow – supposedly Cooke's – and concerned her struggle to maintain the garden left by her husband. With the help of her Indian neighbour she succeeds.

The filming required a great deal of upheaval, as trees had to be removed for access of vehicles; lots of holes were dug and plants – including bananas, but not Abyssinian – were planted.

I think the film would have been better based on Cooke's own life, but it is nonetheless charming.

If anyone has the right to lay claim to being the first exoticist it is certainly Cooke.

much more quickly than with traditional planting;

ii) low maintenance – there are more and more demands on people's time these days, and an exotic garden has minimal maintenance, mostly the time being spent on watering;

iii) year-round appeal – an exotic garden looks little different from winter to summer, bar the splashes of vibrant colour. This is important in a climate where the summers are comparatively short. After all, who would not prefer a lush green winter setting of palms, bamboos and the like to a bleak scene of bare twigs?

ABOVE: Cannas (Indian shot plants) provide splashes of bright colour. This is in the garden of Will Giles, a renowned exoticist living in Norfolk

Gardening fashion

I feel sure that the popularity of what are now referred to as 'hardy exotics' will continue to grow for many years. It has certainly not yet reached its peak.

Other fashions, such as the current one for ornamental grasses, cannot last because they are not diverse enough. On the other hand, hardy exotics – which encompass a vast range of plants from different families, such as palms and bamboos – are mostly bold architectural plants which can be underplanted with the larger-leafed of our

The power of TV

I LIVE IN East London and, when my own garden was featured on BBC2's *Gardeners World* several years ago, 800 people arrived on my open day shortly after. Even now the figure hovers around 300.
I will always remember one visitor, a lady who was the double of Margaret Rutherford. This larger-than-life character appeared at the gate and, after just managing to squeeze through, approached me with walking stick in hand and said, in a bold, upright manner: "This had better be good. I've come all the way from Fulham!" She marched off down the path and disappeared into the undergrowth.
When she eventually reappeared, she was transformed. "Absolutely marvellous. You've worked miracles." As she left, she exclaimed to the waiting queue of 30 or so people: "It's well worth the wait!"

ABOVE: Myles' garden becomes so chocabloc with foliage that visitors can disappear underneath the canopy

The first Chelsea garden

MY AIM IN 1986 was to bring a breath of fresh air to Chelsea. I felt that too many themes had been repeated, from the ubiquitous cottage gardens to the usually overly hard-landscaped ones. I felt that gardening had been in the doldrums for a long time. So, what better way to introduce something new than at Chelsea, the gardening showcase of the world?

Realising that what I planned to stage was very different, I knew that I was going to have to do everything possible to attract the attention of the visitors. Planting alone wouldn't be sufficient, so I decided to include a striking water feature.

Scale was important, and I needed something that would hold its own amid the bold and striking plants. Browsing one afternoon in the Victoria & Albert Museum, I came across a stunning life-size sculpture of Neptune by Bernini. It was perfect! From photographs I created a 10-times life-size copy of just the head and shoulders, which I made painstakingly from chicken wire and cement. The sculpture was three-quarters of a ton and took eight people to lift.

Once placed in the pond it looked as though Neptune had just risen from the depths, spurting water from his mouth, resplendent with trident dripping with seaweed – actually Spanish moss.

It did the trick. Even the Queen, who was behind schedule on her tour of the show and was not planning to visit my garden, stopped in her tracks in surprise!

"Provided exotics are watered sufficiently, specially when first planted, they are more likely to flourish and prosper than dwindle and die"

more familiar herbaceous plants, such as hostas, ligularias, rodgersias and so on.

With their exotic-looking companions, these more traditional plants take on a totally new character.

The practicalities

Green fingers are not essential when gardening with hardy exotics. Provided they are watered sufficiently, specially when first planted, these plants are more likely to flourish and prosper than dwindle and die.

Exotics are, generally speaking, pretty tough subjects seldom prone to bugs and diseases, unlike roses for instance, which have to be sprayed, pruned and dead-headed.

Exotics lend themselves to almost any situation, and look good with buildings – both old and contemporary – in containers, and in gardens of any shape or size.

Non-gardeners can be forgiven for thinking that most of these plants are not hardy or that they are difficult to grow.

It is true, of course, that, until recently, many were thought to be a great deal more tender than they really are; but increasingly mild winters allow us to expand the range of what exotics we can grow.

The microclimates created in towns and cities also enable less hardy plants to be grown.

Though difficult to estimate the number of people hooked on exotic gardening, we know it to be high because of the increase in the sale of these plants.

It is a style which attracts people of all ages and walks of life. The sheer enthusiasim these plants seem to engender, and the pleasure and enjoyment that people appear to have from acquiring them, never ceases to amaze me.

All in all, we have a style which deserves its current high popularity. The attractive nature of the plants seduces even the non-gardener, who perhaps fancies the idea of creating a garden reminiscent of some wonderful holiday in the Mediterranean, or even the Caribbean.

The name 'exoticists', then, has surely been coined to appeal to the followers of this exciting new fashion in gardening.

ABOVE: The Cascade Garden, Myles' medal-winning garden at last year's Chelsea Flower Show, with Apollo as the centrepiece

GROWING EXOTICS
OUTDOORS

Victoriana

Mike Lewington puts an exotic perspective on annuals and bedding plants

Annual' and 'bedding plant' are two loose terms used to describe temporary seasonal plantings. An annual plant is one that germinates, grows, flowers, sets seed and dies within the course of a growing season – normally spring to autumn, but sometimes autumn to spring. Many plants that we think of as annuals are actually frost-tender perennials. The term bedding plant has also changed its usage, originally simply meaning a plant that was large enough to be planted straight into a border.

Many people are rather sniffy about annuals and bedding plants, either regarding them as too much trouble, or considering them to be, well, a bit vulgar.

In the exotic-gardening world, there are basically two types of gardeners – those who like foliage and architectural form and those who like lots of colour. Often the former come to exotic gardens through the palm route and the latter through the tropical shrub route.

This is, of course, a simplification, because even Myles Challis, the epitome of the foliage approach, has brugmansia and hedychium, while tending to blench from a nice big planting of dahlia or solenostemon (coleus).

PICTURES: HARRY SMITH COLLECTION

ABOVE: *Maurandya scandens*

BELOW: Streptocarpus is a favourite of plantsman Christopher Lloyd

But one annual which will appeal to all exoticists of whatever persuasion is *Ricinus communis*. Although technically a tropical shrubby perennial, it shows a perverse reluctance to survive the winter, even under glass, so is best grown as an annual.

This plant produces large lobed leaves and grows to 1.5m (4ft 8in).

Most commonly seen is the coppery-leaved form 'Carmencita', which produces small clusters of red or pink pom-pom flowers. But wellworth growing is 'Gibsonii', which produces particularly large green leaves. Germination takes place from nine days at 20°C, although I

exotica

LEFT: *Cobaea scandens*

RIGHT: Brilliant red pom-poms of *Ricinus communis*

BELOW: *Tradescantia pallida* (purple heart)

> ## "Many plants that we think of as annuals are actually frost-tender perennials"

Grey lightens gloom

While we are on the subject of colour effects, I have noticed that some exotic gardeners overdo the purple and copper foliage, and this can lead to a rather sombre and depressing mood in the garden. A tip from Myles Challis, that I have taken on board, is to lighten such plantings by introducing grey foliage in front, such as *Melianthus major* or *Artemisia arborescens*.

have found viability varies markedly between different commercial sources.

Climbers

The kinds of climbers used to clothe the walls of exotic gardens are, in my view, often rather uninteresting, though valuable in fulfilling their function. Such climbers might include ivies, *Parthenocissus henryana*, *Hydrangea petiolaris* and schizophragma.

Many annual climbers can be used to ramp through these, giving a much needed floral boost. *Ipomoea* 'Heavenly Blue' is commonly seen, but the brilliant red of *I. coccinea* sings out against dark green foliage.

I was most impressed by *I.* 'Star of Yalta', a dark purplish-red, which I first saw growing through Tony Keating's front-garden fence. A more vigorous plant is *I. lobata*, (formerly *Mina lobata*) which has a large Y-shaped flower stalk, with six or eight yellow and red tubular flowers on each fork of the Y. *Ipomoea* germinate in three

ABOVE: *Ipomoea lobata*

LEFT: *Ipomoea tricolor* 'Heavenly Blue'

BELOW: Look for perilla among the herbs

ABOVE: Erect panicles distinguish *Amaranthus hypochondriacus*

to five days at 20°C.

A yet more vigorous plant, with pleasing small arrow-shaped leaves and a profusion of tubular purple flowers all through the summer, is *Maurandya scandens*.

My plant, which lives in a large pot on a sheltered patio, has come through the last two winters unscatheed. Moreover, it does tend to seed itself around, and I often find its slender stems climbing through shrubs and up palms. Germination is at around 10 days at 20°C.

The most vigorous of the 'annual' climbers is *Cobaea scandens*. This Mexican perennial climber, producing 'cup and saucer' flowers, will survive the winter in a sheltered spot.

The species is purple, but a greenish-white form 'Alba' is also available. This climber will easily make 7m (24ft). Germination is at around 10 days at 20°C.

Using bedding

Given that most bedding plants come from South African and South America, they could be considered to be exotic, but I contend that bedding plants need to be used in a different way to the kind of bedding out practised by most gardeners.

Even today, most bedding plants are planted in a pale imitation of Victorian carpet bedding, with alternating colours or bands of colours.

The Victorians developed bedding to a fine art, producing complex patterns, often based on paisley-type shapes. This became known as carpet-bedding, not because it was wall-to-wall, but because the arrangement of colours resembled a Persian carpet. Thus in Victorian times the term bedding became associated with mass seasonal planting.

Unless we have a formal exotic garden, it is unlikely that we would wish to replicate a symmetrical bedding scheme.

Most exotic gardeners wish to create a tropical effect, and this has more to do with a sense of lushness and profusion than with formality.

Augment this sense of lushness by using bedding plants in a different way. Rather than planting alternating clusters of different colours, run large drifts of the same plant through your exotic planting.

Even quite ordinary bedding plants like bush lobelia, usually confined to edging paths, look quite different in a planting over several square yards, giving a sea of dark or pale blue, depending on your fancy, which will keep going to the first frosts.

Favourites

Dip into your wallet and create a large drift of New Guinea strains of impatiens in an area with sufficient shade and moisture.

Where dryness is a problem use *Begonia semperflorens* – not the purple-leaved red-flowered form which I find quite repellent, but the cool and ele-

> ## "In the exotic-gardening world, there are basically two types of gardeners – those who like foliage and architectural form and those who like lots of colour"

LEFT: The gaudy colours of solenostenums will sharpen any border

BELOW: *Rudbeckia* 'Rustic Dwarfs Mixed' is a real joy in a border

"I contend that bedding plants need to be used in a different way to the kind of bedding out practised by most gardeners"

gant green-leaved, white-flowered form.

Whilst in the Dominican republic I noticed *Tradescantia pallida* 'Purpurea' mass-planted under trees. This is a purple-leaved, pink-flowered form of the common house plant.

As it is unlikely to overwinter, you need to have the facilities to propagate it in bulk.

It roots easily from stem cuttings, which can be taken at any time of year. I tried this out last year, and it did not like my heavy clay soil, so a sunny, well-drained site is preferable.

Christopher Lloyd beds out streptocarpus in his exotic garden at Great Dixter, East Sussex. This is another plant which is easy to propagate from midrib cuttings, that is from lateral slices of the leaf. Place in semi-shade in a not too dry position.

A wide range of colours is available from Dibleys Nurseries, tel 01978 790677, catalogue and online ordering on www.dibleys.com.

Apart from their use as floral ground cover, other bedding can be used to provide contrast and colour to plantings of green-foliaged canna and hedychium.

I like to use *Amaranthus hypochondriacus*, a dark red-leaved love-lies-bleeding, but whereas the latter has long floppy inflorescences, the former has erect panicles. It reaches up to 0.6m (2ft), but is smaller in hot dry conditions, where it nonetheless thrives.

Another darker red foliage plant, *Perilla nankinensis*, a Victorian favourite that has largely dropped out of favour, has nicely crinkled edges to the leaves. I like to plant it in groups with *Nicotiana sylvestris*.

Perilla is not easy to find, but can sometimes be located among the herbs on the basis that it is known as the beefsteak plant. Moreover, seed obtained from commercial sources is frequently unviable. If you let your own plants seed you can collect enough for next year. Depending on richness of soil, it will reach between 0.45m and 1.2m (18in and 4 feet).

Rudbeckia 'Rustic Dwarfs Mixed' produces lots of those bronze and mahogany flowers. Rising to 0.6m (2ft), it flowers profusely and for an extended period. I might plant these in front of some purple-leaved cannas as a change from *Dahlia* 'Moonfire'.

I also like to bed out solenostemon in large groups, as does Will Giles in his exotic garden in Norwich.

My own preference is for plants that have large, single-colour leaves, or a large central colour in the leaf, like 'Red Velvet' and 'Walter Turner', rather than plants with small leaves and multiple colours, these giving rather a 'busy' effect.

All in all, it is high time to reinvent bedding and explore its potential in the exotic garden and in modern garden design.

Parks and gardens take note

I wonder whether local authority parks and gardens are going to be producing watered-down Victoriana in the next millenium, or whether a new approach to formal bedding could be considered. It occurred to me that the concept of bedding could be modernised by drawing on the ideas of the Brazilian designer Roberto Burle-Marx, who landscaped Brasilia. He created what were, in effect, abstract paintings, and then planted out the scheme using coloured foliage plants to correspond with the colours in the plan.

The idea of creating asymmetrical or abstract patterns with bedding plants, particularly those with coloured foliage, is an interesting one with which to play around. One could also break with the notion of a harmonious scheme that is easy on the eye and go for extreme colour groupings.

For example, imagine a large yin and yang symbol planted out with the nearly black *Solenostemon* 'Palisandra' on one side and the magenta *Iresine herbstii* 'Brilliantissima' on the other, edged and separated by a gold or grey foliage...

Bamboo bandwagon

Myles Challis sorts out essential bamboos for a hardy exotic garden

Along with all the other hardy exotics with which they associate so happily – palms, tree ferns, phormiums and the like – bamboos have deservedly grown in popularity.

For many years the real potential of bamboos in the garden was not exploited, and as a result their full beauty was not appreciated.

I feel confident now, however, that their time has arrived and that their important role in the formation of the hardy exotic garden will be realised.

Until comparatively recently bamboos were used in gardens only as screening or as 'accent' plants; but their full beauty cannot be fully appreciated when they are mixed with ordinary garden plants.

They need to keep company with other hardy exotics – after all, that is where they belong – their graceful habit rustling with the faintest breeze.

Bamboos are useful for filling corners, diverting paths to create mystery and as a substitute for trees. They are also one of the best subjects for planting at the water's edge where their arching fronds will cast reflections equal in beauty to any weeping willow.

Their huge diversity and range of size and habit means that they suit gardens of any size – some can even be grown in pots.

They range from a few feet tall – some are ideal for ground cover – to impressive towering giants of up to 9m (30ft) in height. Their leaves also vary from only a few inches to more than a foot in length, some being narrow while others are wide, and some with coloured canes (culms) or variegated leaves.

For many years only a few varieties were to be found in garden centres, such as *Pseudosasa japonica* (previously called *Arundinaria japonica*), a rather coarse but tough bamboo with largish leaves, reaching about 3.5m (12ft), and *Fargesia murieliae* and *F. nitida* (both then called arundinaria), with slim canes and small leaves, growing from 1.8-3m (6-10ft). Also to be seen were little bamboos such as *Sasa veitchil* with its bleached leaf tips – a good ground-cover plant, and *Pleioblastus auricomus* (then called *P. viridistriatus*), with its acid-yellow striped leaves – a lovely bamboo for a pot at around a couple of feet.

Wherever grown, it should, however, be trimmed to ground level at the end of each winter to ensure good growth and colour the following season. It likes a sunny position whereas *Sasa veitchil* will tolerate shade.

Choosing bamboos

The beginner could not go wrong with the easily available *Phyllostachys aurea*, a substantial plant between 1.8-4.5m (6-

Arundinaria murialiae syn. fargesia

PICTURES: HARRY SMITH COLLECTION

Pleioblastus viridistriatus

15ft), with yellow-green canes up to about 2.5cm (1in) in diameter and fresh green leaves.

The canes of the strikingly handsome black-stemmed *Phyllostachys nigra* are green at first, maturing to jet black. These two varieties of similar structure have an elegant arching habit and smallish leaves of some 7.5cm (3in).

Semiarundinaria fastuosa is a very upright bamboo growing up to 7.5m (25ft); the young canes mature to a purplish brown and bear 15cm (6in) leaves. Only available from specialist nurseries, this very hardy bamboo is well worth seeking out.

Though the majority of bamboos are tall, there are a few of medium size. *Fargesia spathacea* at around 3m (10ft) is a very elegant plant, with arching canes and delicate leaves. *Fargesir robusta* is a new introduction and of similar character.

By contrast, at around 1.8-2.4m (6-8ft), *Sasa palmata nebulosa* has huge leaves 25-35cm (10-14in) long and up to 10cm (4in) wide, giving it a very distinctive appearance. Though invasive, it can be easily controlled with a sharp spade; alternatively it could be grown in a large pot or tub.

A smaller version of this is *Indocalamus tessellatus* at around 1m (3ft). These have the widest leaves of any bamboo, while some of the narrowest belong to *Pleioblastus linearis*, which grows to around 3.5m (12ft).

Cane characteristics

Chusquea couleou, with distinctive canes bearing 'tufts' of small leaves clustered at the nodes, has perhaps lost some of its earlier glamour since the introduction of many other desirable bamboos.

More beautiful is *Chusquea breviglumis,* with tufts of leaves held on long side branches. Unfortunately, this bamboo needs a huge space in which to develop properly as the canes are widely spaced out and can reach 9m (30ft) in height.

The canes of chusqueas are solid whereas with other bamboos they are hollow.

Large-diameter canes are desirable, of course, but our British climate means that the heavy gauge – and height – of tropically grown bamboos can never be achieved; none the less, some varieties are impressive.

It was at Penjerrick, a sheltered valley garden in Cornwall, that I first encountered a 10.5m (35ft) tall *Phyllostachyus phbescens* with 6cm ($2^{1}/_{2}$in) diameter canes. Sadly, this is not an easy plant to grow as it is somewhat slow.

Phyllostachys bambusiodes at around 6-7.5m (20 to 25ft) is faster growing, but perhaps the best in terms of thick canes and good growth is

Pleioblastus auricomus

Sasa veitchii

"Bamboos are one of the best subjects for planting at the water's edge where their arching fronds will cast reflections equal in beauty to any weeping willow"

Phyllostachys vivax. Given sufficient moisture and shelter, this plant, once established, may produce canes over two inches in diameter and 9m (30ft) high. A specimen of these dimensions has been growing in a Sussex garden for some 30 years.

Phyllostachys viridiglaucescens is another good doer with impressive canes.

Colour

Next to cane thickness and height, colour is fast becoming a desirable feature and there is no shortage of species to choose from. The majority have either plain yellow canes, yellow canes striped green, or green canes striped yellow, and most belong to the phyllostachys group.

Phyllostachys sulphurea 'Robert Young' and *P. aureosulcata* 'Aureocaulis' both have bright golden-yellow canes; *P. a.* 'Spectabilis' has yellow canes striped green; *P. bambusoideds* 'Castillonis' has thick, deep yellow canes with a broad green stripe.

P. aureosulcata and *P. bambusoides* 'Castillonis Inversa' have reversed colour.

Confused: then I recommend *Phyllostachys vivax* 'Aureocaulis' as one of the best, though not the most vigorous, with thick yellow canes striped green.

All these plants grow anything from 4.5-6m (15-20ft) in height.

For something more modest, try two lovely small bamboos with white-striped leaves:

Pleioblastus shibuyanus 'Tsuboi' at (1-1.5m (3-5ft) has subtle creamy-white stripes while *x Hibanobamusa tranquillans* 'Shiroshima' has bolder, more distinctive, striping of the leaves and is taller at 2-3m (6-10ft).

With all this choice there cannot fail to be something to suit every palate. The Japanese have long valued and used the bamboo in their gardens, always in association with water.

Even the smallest plot could accommodate a few of these lovely plants which, along with their foreign cousins, help so much to convey the atmosphere of warmer climates. The hardy palms, tree ferns, cordylines, phormiums, bananas and, not least, the bamboos create a picture which is second to none.

Caring for bamboos

Despite their exotic appearance the majority of bamboos are very hardy plants, some withstanding very low temperatures. Providing they have sufficient moisture especially in the first year after planting, they

Chusquea breviglumis

Phyllostachys nigra

are generally of very easy culture, but they may take four years to become properly established.

Next to drought, their only other dislike is strong wind which can burn the foliage, but some species tolerate this more than others.

Each year bamboos produce a batch of new culms. These usually increase in height annually, some by a few feet or more, until the plant has reached its ultimate height.

The culms live for several years, after which they begin to defoliate, at which time they should be cut out close to ground level, preferably with a sharp saw. Bamboos replenish a percentage of their foliage each year, usually in early summer, just before which they will shed some of their old leaves.

Today, the majority of bamboos available are non-invasive, their canes forming fairly tight clumps which gain in height faster than they spread horizontally, an advantage in small gardens.

If and when they do become too large they can be reduced by cutting off portions, prefer-

Sasa palmata

ably with about six canes. This will require a sharp spade and saw, for, although bamboos are shallow rooted, their root stocks are very tough.

This is a good way of multiplying your plants as you have an 'instant' specimen larger perhaps than you would be able to purchase. Water the clump well before you divide it, and prepare the hole for your new plant with good friable soil

Types of bamboo

There are basically two types of bamboo: those which produce their leaves and branches from the top of the canes downwards, such as pseudosasa, and those which do so from the bottom upwards, such as phyllostachys. The other distinction between them is that the canes of some, like pseudosasa, are permanently clothed with sheaths while others, like phyllostachys are naked — the sheaths quickly falling off — and are, therefore, more attractive especially if coloured or striped.

ABOVE: *Phyllostachys viridi glaucescens*

"The beginner could not go wrong with the easily available Phyllostachys aurea"

LEFT: *Arundinaria nitida syn. fargesia*

that has had a sprinkling of hoof and horn or blood, fish and bone mixed into it. Water in after planting and stake if necessary until it is re-established.

Bamboos appreciate an annual dressing of a fast-release general fertiliser and, because of their shallow roots, plenty of water, especially in summer.

Generally speaking, the short-growing varieties will tolerate shade while the taller ones prefer more open situations. Bamboos flower, though rarely, and can consequently die because the plant expends so much energy in doing so; even if the plant survives, it is often left looking so denuded that it is best removed.

Although only a half dozen or so different bamboos may be found even in a good garden centre, there are now actually nearly 200 varieties in cultivation, and a good number may be found in specialist nurseries.

ABOVE: Cycads growing at
the Kirstenbosch garden in
Cape Town, South Africa
HARRY SMITH COLLECTION

Food of the dinosaurs

Not only do cycads have enormous architectural appeal, as house or conservatory specimens they are among the easiest of plants to care for, says Martin Gibbons

Cycads form a group of ancient, primitive plants which have changed little since the time of the dinosaurs and have been around for at least 250 million years.

Their common name, 'food of the dinosaurs', is based on reality, for they covered great areas of the earth's surface and would have formed an important component in the diet of those giant herbivores.

Man's insatiable appetite for land in the last 100 years has, however, reduced their numbers down to perhaps 1% of the original population as cycads have fallen victim, like so many other plants, to the clearance of huge tracts of land for crop production.

The number of genera has been reduced to 11 and species to just 185 – and we are lucky to have even those.

Realisation of the plight of these primeval plants has resulted in massive worldwide efforts to save those that are left. Natural reserves have been created, and the International Convention on Trade in Endangered Species now makes it an offence to buy or sell them internationally without a permit.

In South Africa every single cultivated plant is microchipped so its every movement can be traced and monitored.

Cycads occur in the wild in

RIGHT: *Encephalartos horridus*

BELOW: *Encephalartos lehmanii*

PICTURES: T. KING

"Cycads have fallen victim like so many other plants to the clearance of huge tracts of land for crop production"

all continents where the climate is reasonably warm, and are particularly frequent in South Africa, Australia, South East Asia and Central America, where the greatest diversity occurs.

The most comonly encountered and much-loved cycad, *Cycas revoluta* – popularly but incorrectly known as the sago palm – comes from the Ryukyu Islands of Japan. The largest genus, encephalartos, with over 50 species, occurs in sub-Saharan Africa and contains some of the most spectacular cycads of all.

Most cycads grow a trunk and sport a crown of stiff green or blue leaves. Their architec-

tural appeal is enormous both for home and garden use. It could be said that they resemble both palms and tree ferns in appearance, but their leaves are invariably much harder and tougher, and botanically speaking they are not even distantly related.

Mature plants produce seeds in cones in the manner of conifers to which they are closer.

Pot grown

For those of us who live far from the tropics, their adaptation to growing in pots means that we can enjoy them too; they can be stood out all summer and moved to a protected spot in the cooler months. A few are even hardy enough to

plant out in the sheltered, temperate garden.

As house or conservatory specimens, cycads are among the easiest of plants to care for. They are tolerant of a whole range of conditions, will often put up with drought, over-watering, dry air and general neglect.

Cycads prefer an open, gritty soil, rich in minerals. Good drainage is essential, together with a generous supply of water especially in hot, dry weather. They need good light and can become 'etiolated' (stretched) if it is too low.

Indoors, the light should be indirect. Outdoors they can become accustomed to full sunlight, and this is probably how they most like to spend the summer, though make sure they don't dry out in warm, dry condtions.

Regular feeding with any house or garden fertiliser will be of benefit, especially during the period of new growth.

Propagation is usually from seed, though basal suckers form on larger specimens and may be removed to produce new plants. Mix the seed with moist compost and place it in a sealed, labelled plastic bag.

Kept in a warm spot, the seeds can germinate very fast; check for white shoots through the plastic. Pot seedlings up in 3 or 4in pots in a mixture as above. Water well initially, thereafter endeavour to keep the soil moist at all times.

Healthy plants are usually pest free and attacks by mealy bug, scale insects or red spider mite are often of a secondary nature; unhappy or unhealthy plants are much more vulnerable. Keep an eye open for these bugs and treat them appropriately before the infestation becomes serious.

Cycas revoluta

Cycas revoluta – named for the rolled or 'revolute' leaf margins – is the most popular cycad for home use. Usually seen as a small potted specimen in the local garden centre, it can grow to a good size over a number of years and will live to a good age, in some countries being passed down from generation to generation.

It is very hardy to cold, and in the UK at least it can certainly be planted out in a sheltered garden.

The base of the plant should be no smaller than, say, a grapefuit, and choose a sunny spot in rich soil. Plant out in late spring or early summer so that the roots can develop during the warmer months.

BELOW: *Cycas revoluta*

In severely cold weather it is a simple matter to drape hessian or an old blanket over the entire plant, removing it after the cold snap. Alas, our summers are often not long enough for the new leaves to be developed and fully hardened before the onset of winter, and they are frequently lost to the first frost.

Your plant can be encouraged to leaf early in the year by placing a clear polythene-covered box over it during spring. This will dramatically raise the temperature and result in advanced growth in plenty of time to mature before the first freeze.

Other cycads
The little known blue-leaved Chinese cycad *Cycas panzhihuaensis* (Panzi cycad) is thought to be one of the most numerous in the world. It is certainly one of the hardiest, taking even severe frosts in its stride, and also one of the fastest growing, Chinese growers reporting 2ft of thick trunk in just five years.

BELOW: *Encephalartos longifolius*

ABOVE: *Macrozamia moorei*
LEFT: *Encephalartos ferox and cone*

At the other end of the scale is the slow-growing *Encephalartos horridus*, from South Africa. It has blue, twisted and extremely spiny leaves as a defence against grazing animals. Its fierce armament has a curious beauty and it is much sought after despite its high price. It is one of a large number of similarly beautiful members of this South African genus.

Others worth a mention are *E. lehmanii* with blue leaves, *E. ferox* with flat and spiny, almost holly-like green leaves, *E. ghellinckii*, very cold hardy, very slow growing, very difficult to find, and *E. woodii*, which was represented in the wild by but a single male plant. No other – or female – plant has ever been found; those in cultivation are from basal suckers.

Some of the most interesting and unusual cycads come from Australia. Bowenia and lepidozamia have just two species each, macrozamia has 25. Easily grown from seed, representatives of these generally all deserve a place in the collection.

This briefest of introductions should serve to whet the appetite of all those who love exotic and unusual plants. But beware, cycads are addictive and an early interest may well turn into a life-long passion.

> ## "In severely cold weather it is a simple matter to drape hessian or an old blanket over the entire plant"

Growth spurts
Cycads have the reputation of being slow growing. This is because all their growth is compressed into a few weeks each year. The rest of the time they seem to be doing nothing, but when the new leaves start to appear, their growth is very fast and they can be seen to change on a daily basis.

During this time of new growth, usually mid summer in the UK, the plant should not be moved; altering its orientation to the light source, usually the sun, can cause the leaves to distort.

RIGHT: *A. victoriae-reginae*

BELOW: *Agave parviflora*

Hardy or half-hardy, agaves and yuccas are versatile garden monsters that offer colour and structure in garden and conservatory, says **Shirley-Anne Bell**

Spiky

Think of architectural plants and among the first that spring to mind are the dramatic, bayonet-shaped leaves and evergreen rosettes of agaves and yuccas, which originated in the Americas.

They are some of the best larger choices to create a Mediterranean or subtropical look, and if you want to make a statement in your garden, these are your exclamation marks.

Because they have such bold forms they are attractive at every stage in their lives. Some are totally hardy, so they offer all-year-round colour and structure in the garden and can be used as stunning cen-

ABOVE: *A. americana* with yellow stripes in the middle of its leaves

trepieces in island beds, to frame openings and as an upright foil to summer bedding schemes.

They will also associate sympathetically with other architectural choices for the ultimate evergreen, low-care garden.

Others are half-hardy, so can double up as striking container subjects for the house or conservatory in the winter. Unlike many container subjects, they are drought-resistant, so need only the minimum of care.

AGAVES

Agaves are distinctive, stemless, rosette-shaped plants. Their long, tapering leaves are stiff and tipped with sharp, needle-like spikes, often margined with spines.

They can be ferocious customers, so should be positioned with care, well away from the edges of paths and

from the attentions of children or pets. For safety's sake the spines can be trimmed back.

As the smaller-growing species can take up to 10 years to flower and the larger ones as many as 40 years, agaves are grown for their foliage.

The best known is *Agave americana*, also known as the century plant because it flowers only when huge – although this does not take 100 years! These are definitely the triffids of the family, as, with time, the plants can reach up to 2m (6ft 6) in height, with a 2-3m (6-10ft) spread and a flower stem of up to 8m (26ft).

Agave americana has dark blue-green leaves, the backs of which are attractively patterned with a ghost-like imprint of the adja-

exclamations

cent leaves, formed as they first unfurled. It is almost hardy in the UK, and will certainly survive in milder or drier areas of the country, especially in a well-drained position.

Furthermore, any slight damage is incidental as the plant grows by replacing its older leaves. Because these are freely offsetting plants, however, some spares can be tucked away in the warm.

Or consider hardy *Agave parryi*, a similar, smaller, species forming compact rosettes up to 80cm (32in), with a grey bloom to its leaves.

Many agaves are grown not only for their spectacular form, but also for their attractive spination. The thread

LEFT: *A. potatorum*

agaves are stunning, with white margins which split away to form an unusual edging of dangling fibres. *Agave filifera*, growing to 65cm (26in) in diameter, is an attractive and borderline hardy species, with long, narrow, glossy green leaves with a thread-like edging.

Agave toumeya, reaching 30 cm (12in) in diameter, and lower-growing *Agave toumeya bella*, have stiff, narrow light green leaves, while *Agave parviflora*, 15 to 25cm (6 to 10in) in diameter, is a lovely miniature, with white markings on the leaves and thread-like edges.

Appealingly squat

Agave potatorum – to 30cm (12in) – is appealingly squat, with fat, very heavily toothed leaves; it also has a choice variegated form.

Agave ferox, a heavily-spined monster, reaching 1m (3ft) across, sports long 2-3cm ($^3/_4$ to 1in) spines on the leaf margins and 9cm ($3^1/_2$in) terminal spines.

Agave macrocantha is a medium-sized and handsome grey-green species, bristling with dark, 3cm- (1in-) long terminal spikes.

If the plants are not to be left outside in the winter, they can be displayed as giant houseplants or they make excellent conservatory subjects. Indeed *A. americana* will spend the winter happily in unheated sheds, greenhouses and outhouses over the winter if kept dry – although they are such showy plants that it is a shame to hide them away!

The variegated agaves are tender, and definitely need winter protection.

Agave americana variegata is

ABOVE: *A. macrocantha*

ABOVE LEFT: *Yucca gloriosa, Y. gloriosa variegata* and *Phormium* 'Yellow Wave' around pond with 'living edge' of hardy succulents

a showier relative of *A. americana*, with broad yellow edges to the leaves. It has an eventual height and spread of 2m (6ft 6), and offsets freely.

Agava americana v. mediopicta is another variegated form, this time with a yellow central stripe and green edges to its leaves; it is slower growing but will reach 2 by 2m (6ft 6 by 6ft 6).

There is also a smart white variegated form, *Agave americana v. mediopicta f. alba*.

Agave stricta is unusual, in that it grows up to 1m (3ft) across and forms large spherical heads of long, thin, tapering leaves, reminiscent of an outsize green bobble on a woolly hat.

Look out, too, for the glorious *Agave victoriae-reginae*, the royal agave, with tightly packed, spineless rosettes of blackish-green leaves, white striped and edged, with black and vicious needle-like spikes on the tips.

Position, propagation

Yuccas are tolerant plants and will grow happily in a sunny position in most UK gardens. Like the agaves, they also make good container subjects, although they do not need winter protection. They can be propagated in the spring, either by root cuttings or by dividing up larger plants. Because many species grow rapidly from seed, you can also extend your range quite easily and cheaply.

ABOVE: Root cuttings of *Yucca filamentosa*

Stylish winters

The less hardy species are best kept in large containers, where they make dramatic focal points. Try them on patios and alongside paths and steps. Use them to set off a smart front door or to brighten up dull areas.

They lend themselves particularly well to mixed summer planting, where they can act as a striking centrepiece, surrounded by flowering bedding plants.

Try, for example, *Agave americana variegata* with clear blue pansies, or a plainer cousin with flame-red pelargoniums.

After the summer plants have finished, these containers will transform into enormously stylish house or conservatory plants to brighten up the colder months.

Planting, propagating

Agaves appreciate rich but well-drained compost, and will grow vigorously if fed and watered well in the summer, though they will tolerate drought happily.

In the spring and summer plants can be increased from the tiny plantlets that sucker up around the base. Use a sharp knife to separate each one from the thickened root attaching it to its parent, and pot it up separately.

Suckering can be increased in potted subjects if you choose a shallow, bowl-like container; then the babies will head upwards rapidly around the edges of the pot.

Agaves also grow well from seed – apart from the variegated forms which can only be propagated from cuttings.

YUCCAS

Yuccas are dramatic evergreen plants which are available as stemless rosette-shaped forms or as small trees with stout

"Agaves can be ferocious customers, so should be positioned with care, well away from the edges of paths and from the attentions of children or pets"

ABOVE: *A. americana v. mediopicta*

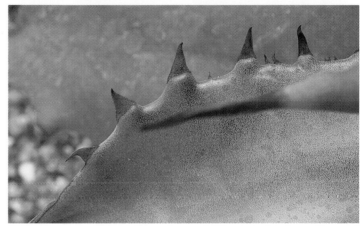

ABOVE: *Agave ferox* spine – keep children and pets well away!

trunk-like stems. They produce dramatic spikes of bell-shaped white flowers and are hardy in the UK.

Yucca gloriosa, or the Spanish dagger, is a fully-hardy garden variety reaching up to 2.5m (8ft). Initially it grows as a large rosette, with stiff, pointed, spine-tipped blue-green leaves. It becomes tree-like with age, forming a stout trunk once the lower leaves die, when they can be removed with a sharp downwards tug.

Yucca gloriosa variegata is the showy, variegated form, with bright pink, yellow and green leaves when small, maturing to green edged with gold.

The plants are free-flowering in midsummer to autumn, bearing magnificent spikes, 1m (3ft) or more high, with pendant, tulip-shaped flowers which are reddish on the outside and cream inside.

Yucca flaccida is a stemless species, reaching up to 75cm (30in), with arching, rosette-forming green leaves. This also has dramatic variegated forms, like *Yucca flaccida variegata*, with bright yellow edging to the softly drooping leaves, and a reversed form, 'Golden Sword', with a broad, golden mid-stripe and green-edged leaves.

Yucca filamentosa, or Adam's needle, is another

ABOVE: *Agave americana* keeping company in a gravel garden with *Aeonium zwartkopf* and *Aeonium arboreum*

ABOVE: Winter hardy –
Agave americana in snow

LEFT: *Yucca gloriosa variegata* flower spike

ABOVE: *A. toumeya*

attractive stemless species, reaching 2m (6ft 6) in height. It has a 1.5m (5ft) spread, with erect greyish-green leaves edged with a multitude of curling white threads, and carries tall panicles of tulip-shaped flowers in middle to late summer. This also has a spectacular variegated form, 'Bright Edge'.

Other yuccas to look out for include *Y. whipplei*, a stemless, globular clump-forming species, reaching up to 1m (3ft) high, with long, narrow, stiff leaves with a glaucous grey finish. Also note *Y. glauca*, another grey-green species, *Y. elata*, which has long, thin thickened leaves, and *Y. intermedia*, with rosettes of long, thin stiff leaves.

You may also come across half-hardy *Yucca elephantipes*, sold as a houseplant or as that infamous foreign holiday souvenir, the 'stick in a bag', which is actually an easily-rooted section of the slender woody trunk.

This makes an exotic palm-like tree for the house or conservatory, forming a clump of densely-branched stems with stiff, pointed green leaves. It can, however, quickly outgrow its space – it reaches 10m (33ft) in habitat!

In the glasshouse we have a large specimen which is cut down regularly – and brutally – whenever it reaches the roof. Moreover, cuttings that we have planted outside have proved to be completely hardy so far.

LEFT: *Agave americana variegata* in urn

Architectural complements

To reinforce the architectural effect of agaves and yuccas, consider the following hardy evergreen choices:
Trachycarpus fortunei (Chinese windmill palm) – stiff, fan-like leaves and slim, solitary trunk – very cold tolerant; cordylines (New Zealand lily palm, Cornish/Torquay palm) – dramatic, fast-growing 'surrogate palms' with bayonet-like leaves – plain green *C. australis* or colourful forms like 'Red Star' and 'Purple Tower'; phormiums (New Zealand flaxes) – grown for their bold, sword-shaped leaves and fabulous colours, such as variegated pinks, creams and purples – large growing varieties can make huge architectural subjects while dwarf forms are ideal container plants.

Banana drama

So long as you don't expect them to fruit, bananas can be grown outside – even in the chilly UK, says Myles Challis

Musa basjoo

MYLES CHALLIS

If asked which plants come to mind when thinking of an exotic holiday abroad, most people would probably say palm trees and bananas. Because these two plants are naturally associated with warmer climates, however, many believe that they are impossible to grow in the UK.

Tell the average person in the street that you can grow bananas in the cool climate of Britain and you would get a look of disbelief along with a challenge to prove it. Of course, when I say bananas I mean without the fruit; our climate is too cool and our summer too short for that.

Any exoticist will tell you that despite the seeming odds it is perfectly possible to grow banana plants here. They have been growing here for many years in some Cornish and Gulf Stream gardens and there is even an old clump at The Royal Horticultural Society's Wisley gardens.

The best position in the garden for bananas is a sunny one sheltered from strong wind as their large papery leaves catch every eddy and are unsightly if they become lacerated, but if undamaged they will be the most imposing plants in your garden. Bananas require a rich soil and copious watering in the summer months. A generous mulching of well-rotted cow manure or a once-weekly liquid feed will give good results.

In my many years of growing a vast range of plants both under glass and outdoors the banana has remained my firm favourite. I became hooked on large-leaved plants at a very early age, starting with hot-house plants and later outdoors, initially with plants like *Gunnera manicata*.

"The best position in the garden for bananas is a sunny one sheltered from strong wind as their large papery leaves catch every eddy"

Striving as I always was to create an ever-increasing exotic picture led me inevitably to bananas.

Bananas grown under glass, *see below*, will need some shading in the summer months to prevent scorching, and the humidity should be kept high. If the temperature gets above 29.5°C, ventilation should be effected.

If you are yet to buy your first banana plant then I would certainly suggest you start with *Musa basjoo, see below*. If you can find a sheltered nook for it you will be more than pleased with the results.

In time it will form a clump of several plants, *see panel*.

In the garden bananas are essential to complete the tropical feel. Their great sails will rise in ever-increasing height as the summer progresses, casting deep shadows and swaying with the gentlest breeze.

Like all hardy exotics, bananas look their finest when they are in company with their kindred kind.

Hardy palms, cordylines, tree ferns and phormiums will all contrast and compliment each other and of course set off your bananas to the best effect. You can then sit out in the summer months and imagine you are in some far off tropical paradise where the summer never ends.

Musa basjoo

The so-called hardy Japanese banana, *Musa basjoo*, is the hardiest banana known at present, although there are other contenders waiting in the wings. It is true of course that the majority of the banana species, including the common banana *Musa x paradisiaca*, are tropical plants requiring both heat and humidity, meaning that they are strictly greenhouse plants for us here in Britain. For sheer square yardage of leaf, bananas beat all other plants in the vegetable kingdom, are vigorous growers

HARRY SMITH COLLECTION

ABOVE: *Musa acuminata* **'Dwarf Cavendish'**...

RIGHT: ... for fruit grow *Musa acuminata* **in the greenhouse**

HARRY SMITH COLLECTION

and are some of the handsomest plants to be found.

Musa basjoo can be grown anywhere but in the coldest parts of Britain provided it is given winter protection by wrapping it in straw or some other insulating material. Even balmy Cornwall can experience sharp frosts and, while this

plant will tolerate a few degrees without protection, a severe frost will cut it to the ground.

Being root-hardy, it will regenerate from the base if this happens, but if large plants are desired then protection will be necessary.

In late-autumn-early-winter, when the first frosts begin, cut off the leaves and wrap the trunk, preferably with a 10cm (4in) layer of straw. This can be held in place with a column of chicken wire supported with a large bamboo cane.

Then cover this with a plastic sleeve – it is essential to keep the straw dry. Remember to make a few small vertical slits in the plastic to prevent condensation. When the plants begin to push forth in the spring remove everything and store for use the following winter.

By this method your plants will soon reach full size – anything from 3-5½m (10-18ft) depending on where you live.

Ensete ventricosum

Musa basjoo satisfied my needs until I discovered the fabulous Abyssinian banana, Ensete ventricosum (previously called Musa ensete). Though not hardy this is a far more beautiful plant which, because of its stout trunk and fleshy leaves which have a thick, prominent red midrib, stands up to the wind much better than Musa basjoo.

No doubt its structure is due to the fact that it originates from the lower slopes of the Abyssinian mountains where it grows as high as the 7,000ft contour.

This plant flourishes in the open air in the summer months here in Britain and is one of the fastest-growing plants I have ever come across. Originally it was only available as seed but

ABOVE: Musa makes a dramatic border plant...

RIGHT: ... and is wonderful inside too.

now most of the specialist nurseries have it.

If, however, you wish to try it from seed, you will find them relatively easy to germinate in a propagator or under glass at about 21°C. Once the seed has germinated, the young plants

Musa velutina

Growing from offsets

Offsets (suckers) – young plants that are produced around the parent plant – can be separated if desired. They are best left until they have 2-3ft 0.6-1m of trunk, by which time they have a reasonable root system.

They should be separated with a sharp spade, cutting as close to the parent plant as possible. Alternatively cut through but leave the offset in the ground for three to four weeks; this shouold stimulate the offset into producing more root.

Lift your offset and put it into the smallest pot that will accommodate it. When the pot has filled with root, the plant can then be planted in the border. If and when a banana plant fruits it will then die but in the process produce several offsets (suckers) to replace itself.

The only exception to this rule is the Abyssinian banana which is why it is usually grown from seed.

HARRY SMITH COLLECTION

Ensete 'Maurelii'

MYLES CHALLIS

are fast growing and can reach 0.6 or 1m (2-3ft) in six months.

Re-pot them frequently and water and feed regularly while growing vigorously. This treatment will produce plants 2 to 3 metres high in 18 months.

In my own garden I have grown this plant up to 6m (20ft) high, the leaves measuring 4 by 0.7m (14 by 2.5ft). At this size it is the most impressive plant that can be grown outside in the British Isles, albeit only for the summer months.

Abyssinian bananas should not be put outside until all risk of frost is past. Watering should be moderate until the rate of growth increases.

Young plants up to about 1½m (5ft) should be grown in containers, after which they are best planted out in the border.

In summer large plants especially will need copious watering to compensate for the evaporation from their huge sails; as

with all bananas, feed regularly.

Plants take several years to reach maximum size – about 6m (20ft) in the UK, but become rather unmanageable in this state. Unless you have some strong helpers to hand it is better to replace these

Ensete ventricosum

MYLES CHALLIS

"Bananas grown under glass will need some shading in the summer months"

plants with younger, smaller ones when this happens.

In late autumn, before the first frosts, move your plants to their winter quarters. Open-ground plants should be lifted and the rootball reduced to fit into as small a pot as possible; remember to put some drainage material in the bottom first.

To remove water which collects in the leaf bases, tip the plant on its side to remove water, pot up and fill around the roots with some fine, friable soil. If your plants are too tall for your greenhouse or conservatory cut off all the leaves – most of their height is made up of their leaves.

Abyssinian bananas are very susceptible to root rot in the winter months when they are more or less dormant, so watering should therefore be completely withheld until they begin to make perceptible growth in the spring when moderate watering can begin. A minimum winter temperature of 7-10°C is best.

Despite the trouble involved in over-wintering these plants, you will be more than rewarded with a spectacular summer display.

Other varieties

Arguably even more beautiful is the dark red-leafed form called Ensete 'Maurelii' (previously called *Musa maurelii*). It is sometimes incorrectly listed by some nurseries as *Ensete* 'Rubra'.

The entire undersides of the leaves of this ravishing plant are deep maroon or purple while their upper surfaces are often flushed the same colour.

A few years ago a form of *Musa basjoo* appeared, reputedly from the far off Russian island of Sakhalin, north of Japan. If this is the case it should prove to be even hardier than the present form in cultivation, but only time will tell. It has been seen growing well in a Belgian garden where it is given winter protection.

Another species new on the scene, which should prove reasonably hardy, is *Musa sikkimensis* syn. *M. hookeri*.

If this is so it will be preferable to *Musa basjoo* because the leaves are of thicker texture, so offering more wind resistance. The leaves and fruit are also flushed purple.

Of smaller stature at 1.8-2.4m (6-8ft), and more com-

ED GABRIEL

ABOVE: *Ensete Ventricosum* on display at Tatton last year

pact, is *Musa* 'Rajapuri'. This plant, though hailing from India, grows at high altitude so should also prove hardy given winter protection in situ.

The same should apply to *Musa* 'Orinoco', a taller plant. Both these varieties produce small edible fruit.

Musa velutina is a small-growing species which produces pinkish-mauve flower and bananas. Again, if protected, it should survive. I saw it once in a cold north-Cornish garden.

If fruit rather than foliage is what you want then *Musa acuminata* 'Dwarf Cavendish' (formerly *Musa cavendishii*) is the one to grow. This strictly greenhouse variety is a very stocky, freely suckering plant growing 1.8-2.4m (6-8ft) high.

It produces large hands of medium-sized very tasty bananas. Though bearing larger fruit, the common banana, *Musa x paradisaca*, is much too tall for all the biggest greenhouses.

Purely ornamental is *Musa zebrina*, another greenhouse variety of medium size 1.8-2.4m (6-8ft). This is a very striking plant in that the leaves have a beautiful burgundy marbling

HARRY SMITH COLLECTION

LEFT: *Musa acuminata*

A tree echium enhances the exotic feel of this *Dicksonia antarctica*

CHRIS SKARBON

"Fossils hundreds of millions of years old have been found, and they would certainly have been food for many of the 'veggy' dinosaurs"

Ballast
from the past

Loved by the Victorians, who kept them in conservatories, tree ferns are now subjects for the exotic garden. **Myles Challis** has his favourites…

BACKGROUND PICTURE:
Cyathea dealbata is another tender customer but worth growing for the silver-white undersides of its fronds

Of the many plants that we can use in exotic gardening, the tree ferns must surely rank as some of the most beautiful. And the best in terms of hardiness, *Dicksonia antarctica*, a fully fronded specimen usually over 2m (7ft) across especially if situated by water, is a magnificent sight indeed.

Tree ferns are extremely ancient plants. Fossils hundreds of millions of years old have been found, and they would certainly have been food for many of the 'veggy' dinosaurs as would the cycads, a race of equally ancient plants.

Ferns in general were extremely popular in Victorian times. The first nurseries specialising in them were established to cater for the

These three *Dicksonia antarctica* at Trebah Garden, near Falmouth in south Cornwall, served as ballast on returning packet boats in the 1880s and were among the first to be planted in the UK

CHRIS SKARBON

BELOW: Tender *Cyathea cooperi* looks handsome in a container and can be brought indoors should frost threaten

HARRY SMITH COLLECTION

huge demand, and most large conservatories or 'winter gardens' housed collections of them.

Some of the first *Dicksonia antarctica* to be planted outside in the British Isles arrived as ballast on packet ships in the 1880s. These were planted in several balmy Cornish gardens including for example Trebah. They thrived in the mild climate, even seeding themselves around, and became a familiar sight.

And there they remained until comparatively recently when a few adventurous people like myself began experimenting with them in less favourable conditions, protect-

ing them in the winter months sometimes with bales of straw.

Then around 1992 Pantiles nursery in Chertsey, Surrey began importing container loads of *Dicksonia antarctica* trunks from Tasmania. These had been rescued from areas where the forest was being cleared. They proved hardier than their Australian cousins and could be grown without lots of protection – but a handful of straw placed in the crown is still a wise precaution.

Others followed suit and the trunks are still being imported, though now from Australia which means they may not be quite as hardy as the Tasmanian originals which are

identifiable by their particularly thick trunks – usually an indication of a slower growth rate.

Dicksonias gain only an inch or so of trunk a year so tall specimens can be hundreds of years old.

Tree fern choices

Dicksonias, usually referred to as **Tasmanian** tree ferns, arrive as logs, having had their fronds removed, and are sawn off at the base, leaving the rootball behind. But these trunks are in fact a mass of fibrous root, so the portion buried in the ground – normally a foot – will start, though slowly, to form a 'new' rootball.

It is important when first planting these trunks to keep them moist, especially through spring and summer when they will produce a whole set of a dozen or more new fronds all at once.

They should be watered at the top in the crown and the

> ## "Dicksonias gain only an inch or so of trunk a year so tall specimens can be hundreds of years old"

MYLES CHALLIS

ABOVE: *Dicksonia antarctica* set among cannas and geraniums by Leyhill Prison at a Chelsea Flower Show

"The fronds can reach two metres in length and very old plants can be several metres high"

trunk should be sprayed as well as the surrounding soil. When growing it will also benefit from a dilute feed of seaweed-based fertiliser.

These plants prefer a position in dappled shade out of strong wind. Although fine planted individually, if you have space a group of three of different sizes is particularly attractive.

The fronds can reach two metres in length and very old plants can be several metres high.

Of similar size and hardiness but with slightly shorter, lighter green fronds is **Dicksonia fibrosa**, the 'golden' tree fern from New Zealand, which has a light brown trunk of equal thickness to *D. antarctica*. Unless you are a collector there is not much point in including it.

The same, however, cannot be said of **Dicksonia squarrosa** , the 'Westland' or 'Weiki'

tree fern also from New Zealand. This differs substantially in having a slender black trunk, with fronds which grow in a much flatter plain. These are dark green 2m (7ft) long on dark petioles (stems).

The other distinction is that this plant is less frost hardy, and while it tolerates about -5°C it is best brought under cover in severe weather. Alternatively it makes a good frost-free conservatory plant. Generally speaking the more slender the trunk the more tender the species of tree ferns.

While I would recommend *Dicksonia antarctica* first and foremost as being the best for its beauty and hardiness, especially for the novice, my personal favourite among the

RIGHT: Evening light filters through the delicate tracery of the *D. antarctica* crown fronds

Protection and care

CHRIS SKARBON

Remember that despite the fact that we are experiencing milder winters, climatic conditions can vary greatly from one area to another. The size of your tree fern also makes a big difference, so avoid buying small plants wherever possible as these are less hardy than adult plants. Otherwise give them winter protection until they are larger.

Tree ferns are generally quite expensive so it is worth being prepared to protect them from the weather. The crown is the most vulnerable part of the plant but is the easiest to protect. Straw pushed down into it will help tremendously, and a slate held in place over the straw to help keep it dry will improve its function.

In severe frost even *Dicksonia antarctica* will lose its fronds but this will not harm the plant. A few layers of Agrifleece thrown over the fronds affords moderate protection. If you live in a very cold area but want to try a tree fern – and who could blame you? – I would suggest you pack a thick layer of straw around the trunk as well as protecting the crown. For anyone who is trying a cyathea for the first time I would recommend you to do the same.

Newly planted *Dicksonia antarctica* bought as logs produce very large fronds the first year but smaller ones thereafter. If your plant is producing very small, rather stunted fronds, the most likely reason is insufficient water at the crown.

Cyatheas on the other hand produce rather small fronds the first year and larger ones from then on. Incidentally, while it is perfectly OK for a dicksonia to have no rootball when you purchase it, a cyathea must have one as it is dependent on it to survive. Most good nurseries ensure this when buying them but it is best to check.

Generally speaking, tree ferns are easy to grow given sufficient moisture and, unlike common hardy ferns, appreciate feeding as well.

CHRIS SKARBON

ABOVE: *Cyathea australis* crown – the fronds will grow back
LEFT: Tree ferns growing in New Zealand

tree ferns is the spectacular 'black' tree fern or 'Mamaku' from New Zealand, **Cyathea medularis**. Although not hardy in that it will only tolerate very light frost, it grows very well outside in the summer months, enjoying the fresh air.

The crown consists of fewer fronds than on the dicksonia, but they are much broader and up to 6m (20ft) in length, and dark green. The fat unfurling croziers covered in black scales born atop a slender black trunk are a wonderful sight.

This very fast-growing tree fern requires frequent repotting and copious watering in summer. Providing you have the space it ultimately needs it will prove a showstopper.

Several large plants grew on the Isle of Tresco until an unusually bad winter wiped them out, but a specimen survives outside a garden in

south-west Ireland.

Cyatheas should never have water poured on their crowns as this can cause rot, but their roots should never be allowed to dry out.

The hardiest of the cyatheas is **C. australis**, the rough tree fern from Australia. It is a robust plant with a substantial trunk – for a cyathea – with a large crown – even when young – of metallic-green fronds on rough stalks.

Although it is known to tolerate some frost, its scarcity in the UK means that its exact level of hardiness is not yet known, but its main advantage over other tree ferns is its toleration of full sun providing it has sufficient moisture at the roots.

This plant is sometimes confused with **Cyathea cooperi**, which is a much more tender species, with a much more slender trunk and, importantly,

soft, smooth scales unlike the very rough trunk of *C. australis*. None-the-less, it is a very nice plant for the conservatory or frost-free greenhouse.

Cyathea dealbata, the 'silver' tree fern, the national symbol of New Zealand, has fronds up to 3m (10ft) in length which are silver-white underneath. Like *C. cooperi* it will only stand minimal frost so is another contender for the greenhouse.

High altitude usually means hardiness and this should be the case with **Cyathea dregei** which grows at up to 2000m in its native South Africa. It is reputed to tolerate temperatures as low as -12°C. Though not a large-growing species it is rather distinctive in having very upright fronds which give it a cycad-like appearance.

Garden hardiness

The number of different tree ferns becoming available is growing all the time due to the increasing interest in exotics in general, indicating the need for continued experimentation to discover their garden-worthi-

ness, especially in terms of hardiness.

In the exotic garden tree ferns are a must for damp and shady areas and especially by water. In the wild they often appear in gullies and by rivulets.

They associate well with all other hardy exotics, their lush leafy fronds always gaining admiration and comment, and quite understandably of late they have become one of the most popular and widely sought after of all these plants.

"A cyathea must have a rootball as it is dependent on it to survive"

Thriving in
dark corners
and providing
evergreen
ground cover,
hardy ferns are
perfect for
those hard-to-
grow-anything
areas, says
Martyn Graham

LEFT:
Dryopteris

PICTURES: HARRY
SMITH COLLECTION

Primal
species

Few plants suggest the
primeval quite like
the fern. These mod-
est plants have been growing since the Jurassic and,
having survived dinosaurs,
they certainly must be hardy
evergreens.

Ferns can be planted in
between or in front of other
plants, in containers as part
of a mixed planting or in winter baskets to add a touch of
the exotic to a cold day.

Favourite ferns

The ferns that I recommend below often have many different types (cultivars). If you feel like making a serious collection of them, it may well be worth contacting a specialist nursery – the basic types featured in this article can be obtained from any well-stocked garden centre.

Asplenium scolopendrium The heart's tongue fern is native to England and grows both in dry and wet conditions. Depending on the cultivar, it can grow up to 60cm (24in) tall and prefers alkaline soil. Some varieties are tall and thin, others wide with serrated edges, whilst some, like 'Golden Queen', have bright yellow foliage

Blechnum chilense This South African fern, like all blechnums, prefers acid soil and is happy in both dry and wet conditions. This blechnum has two different leaf types; the horizontal ones close to the ground are sterile while the erect ones are fertile

Blechnum spicant This fern is native to England and can grow up to 45cm (18in) in height; its pinnate leaves have a particularly exotic appearance. This fern grows in similar conditions to *Blechnum chilensis*

Cyrtomium fortunei The iron fern takes its name from the Greek word for curved, which refers to the fern's leaf shape. It prefers a damp shady position but will grow in the sun if kept well watered. The resultant plant will have an improved appearance if grown in neutral or acid soil

Dryopteris Whilst most ferns of this group are not evergreen, some keep a few leaves during the winter. *Dryopteris erythrosora* and *Dryopteris fuscipes*, whose leaves change colour from pink to red to green, both grow to 60cm (nearly 2ft) tall, and could well be worth trying

Polypodium australe As the fronds of this Australian fern emerge in August, they remain especially fresh during the winter. Australe is the least hardy of the polypodiums, and prefers a wetter position.

Polystichium setiferum The soft shield fern is native to the UK and grows to a height of about 90cm (36in). An interesting cultivar, *Polystichium proliferum plumosa densum*, generally prefers a moist alkaline soil and has rust brown as well as green leaves during the winter. In harsh weather the fronds can be protected by fleece

Polypodium vulgare Unlike most ferns the liquorice fern prefers dry soil. Both polypods grow to about 38cm (15in) high

"The acidity or chalk content of soil can dramatically affect a fern's growth"

Most ferns prefer moist, but not boggy, growing conditions though, generally speaking, evergreen varieties tend to favour drier rather than wetter locations; this is particularly true in winter when water-logged ground can easily kill many plants.

One advantage of the fern is that it prefers shade for much

of the day; as a result, if you have a dark corner where attempts to grow much else have failed, you will probably find a fern that will thrive there.

ABOVE LEFT: *Blechnum chilense*

LEFT: *Asplenium scolopendrium*

ABOVE: *Polypodium australe*

"If you have a dark corner where attempts to grow much else have failed you will probably find a fern that will thrive there"

Caution should also be used when moving a plant from a relatively shady location to a sunnier one as the fern's fronds (leaves) can easily be burnt by the sun. Gradually exposing the ferns to increasing amounts of sunlight over the course of a month will reduce the chance of leaf damage.

Finally, bear in mind that unless a very short fern is being grown, excessively windy situations should be avoided to prevent wind damage to the fronds.

Soil pH
The acidity or chalk content of soil can dramatically affect a fern's growth, so care should

be taken to choose the right fern for the soil's pH value.

For example, blechnums and *Polypodium vulgares* prefer acid soil. If grown in chalky soil, the leaves will turn yellow and either grow poorly or die. One remedy is to add Sequestrene to the soil, or to grow the plants in ericaceous compost which compensates for the iron deficiency that causes the yellowing.

Ferns that prefer a chalky site are *Asplenium scolopendrium*, *Polypodium australe* and polystichums.

All ferns like growing in soil that contains plenty of organic matter. If you want your ferns

to spread their root systems, or spread their spores around the mother plant, a mulch of compost is in order; this will also keep the soil moist and free draining.

Fertilising
Very young ferns do not benefit from being fertilised – there may be too much top growth at the expense of building up an adequate root system. Older ferns, however, are worth taking the time to fertilise.

If time permits, regular liquid feeding is the best method, though slow-release fertilisers have proved adequate alternatives.

Where to plant
Where possible avoid positioning a fern where it will be exposed to the sun during the hottest hours of the day.

Ferns growing in pots probably need more fertilising than those in the ground, and certainly need more watering.

Propagation

Polypodiums make particularly good groundcover plants, but in truth many ferns whose spores germinate readily will also do the job. If you want to grow a lot of ferns for this purpose, propagation through their spores is the best method.

Spores of most ferns turn black or brown around July – they can be seen underneath the leaves. Once collected, the spores can be sown in pots in a compost previously sterilised with boiling water some hours beforehand. Sterilisation avoids any stray seedlings germinating at the same time as the fern spores.

The seed trays or pots should then be sealed in plastic bags in order to maintain adequate humidity. When the seedlings are large enough they can be grown on in 3in pots – though it may take several years to reproduce reasonable size ferns using this method.

Cloning

Generally speaking, the plants produced using the method described above will not be identical to the parent plant – though you may end up with an improved version.

If you want to produce an identical plant to that of the parent, you must use vegetative propagation methods.

Some ferns, such as polypodiums, can have their roots cut into sections with a growing bud on it and potted up. The growing crowns of mature ferns can be divided to produce several new larger ferns.

Ferns often form bulbils on their fronds. By severing a frond full of these ripe brown bulbils and pegging it onto a tray of soilless compost, new ferns can be raised. The compost should be adequately watered, and the tray sealed inside a plastic bag. This can then be left in a warm, light location until they have rooted. They can subsequently be grown on in 3in pots.

Protecting

Luckily outdoor ferns don't suffer much from insect attack. Vine weevil can occasionally be a problem and can be treated with a specialised insecticide.

In very wet conditions some

ABOVE LEFT: *Cyrtomium fortunei*

ABOVE: *Polypodium vulgare*

ferns can be attacked by fungi – though this can normally be contained by using a proprietary fungicide.

"If you want to produce an identical plant to that of the parent you must use vegetative propagation methods"

Growing Exotics

Under Glass

The viable option

Mike Lewington debates the pros and cons of propagating seed bought from specialist suppliers

The first issue we have to address is whether it is worthwhile growing exotics from seed, given that there are now so many nurseries and garden centres selling mature exotic plants. After all, isn't it much easier to buy a nice plant, rather than go through all the palaver of trying to germinate them, nurse them through the seedling stage, and then wait a couple of years until the plants reach a reasonable size?

At this point, I am sure that you are expecting me to start talking in a misty-eyed way about the profound pleasures of seeing a tiny shoot poke its head above the potting compost. I don't deny that I get a

lot of pleasure from successful germination, but in the long run it is the mature plant that we are after, and the route there should not be an end to itself.

There are some very good reasons for growing plants from seed. The first is that this may be the only form of propagation possible – this is true for annuals and biennials, but also for some perennials. The second reason is that it is cheap, especially if you want a lot of them. The third reason is that the plants may not be available in this country.

On the down side, seed-raised plants may be very inferior to named forms. For example, it is very easy to raise large numbers of *Canna indica* from seed. In their first season these

Brugmansia x candida 'Knightii'

will flower as 46cm (18in) plants. However, the flowers will be much smaller and of poorer colour than a named form which has been selected and then vegetatively propagated.

Other down sides relate to unusual plants. Suppliers shift popular seeds quickly, whereas other seed can be hanging around their seed bank for years, with a corresponding

drop in viability. Moreover, many seed companies rely on individuals in various parts of the world to supply them from their own collections or from indigenous sources. They are to a large extent taking it on trust that the seeds are what they say they are, and this is not always the case.

Moreover, species normally breed true in the wild, usually

Iochroma australe

HARRY SMITH COLLECTION

Hardy or not?

Silverhill Seeds assure us that *Aloe broomii*, pictured opposite, is easy to grow from seed but warn us that it is quite a large species and may not like hothouses.

> "I prefer to have plants in my garden that visitors have never seen before, or that would-be players of Competitive Botany get hopelessly wrong"

ED GABRIEL

HARRY SMITH COLLECTION

ABOVE: Try raising aloes, like this *A. broomii*, from seed

Aloe vera

because they are incompatible with other species found in the same locality. So in most cases wild-collected seed will be true, which is why there is such a high premium on seed with a collector's number. However, if the seed is collected from a garden, or from a collection where there is open pollination, and where there are species from different localities, then hybridisation may occur.

Seeds from abroad

On the plus side, though, purchasing seed from abroad is considerably cheaper and easier than buying plants, given the shipping charges and phytosanitary certification. Many foreign seed companies realise that the UK is a major market and thus will accept cheques from UK banks.

One such is Silverhill Seeds of Cape Town, which has an extensive list, much of which is collected from the wild. Of particular interest to exoticists is the fact that they list *Melianthus major*, which is

Seeds on the web

For anyone who is interested in developing a collection from seed, B&T World Seeds offer a valuable resource, with more than 40,000 different species.

Their website offers the facility of downloading particular lists, or you can purchase their 'Seedy ROM', which gives the full Master List with detailed plant descriptions.

Apart from pursuing possibly hardy aloes, I am also interested in possibly hardy agaves, and looked up agave on the Seedy ROM to find more than 100 different types; in many cases the same species is offered collected from a range of different named sites. This is very useful from our point of view, because some areas may have higher winter rainfall, so populations of that species from those areas may be more resistant to UK rainfall levels.

B&T World Seeds also offer a dozen species of the Andean genus puya, some species of which produce flower spikes of strange metallic blues. Some species are proving hardy in London, especially if planted sideways into a bank, or through an inch or two of gravel.

Most exotics of tropical or subtropical origin germinate easily at temperatures of 21°C, but puya, however, germinate in late autumn from a winter sowing in a cold frame, suggesting that they need a cold period followed by a warm period, and then germinate as the temperatures fall.

B&T World Seeds also have a range of unusual – in the sense that I've never seen them – trachycarpus including *T. latisectus*, *T. martianus*, with collections from the Khasia Hills, and from Nepal, *T. princeps* and *T. takil*.

Now this illustrates one of the good things about growing plants from seed, which is that you could easily buy this lot for a couple of quid, and assuming you successfully germinated them, and trachycarpus is not difficult to germinate, you would then have a nice collection of rare palms.

Trachycarpus fortunei look their best in a truly exotic garden like Trebah in Cornwall

CHRIS SKARBON

HARRY SMITH COLLECTION

HARRY SMITH COLLECTION

LEFT: *Melianthus major* is also called honey flower

BELOW: *Datura inoxia*

HARRY SMITH COLLECTION

frequently difficult to obtain as a plant in the UK.

Incidentally, *Melianthus major* is one of those seeds which seems to germinate better when subjected to variations in day and nighttime temperatures. I have found that germi-

nation is far better if the seeds are sown and then left on the greenhouse bench rather than put in a propagator.

Silverhill Seeds also list four other species of melianthus, which are little known in UK cultivation, although, as they

have much smaller, green leaves, they are rather less garden-worthy.

Their extensive list of succulents includes more than 80 species of aloe, including *A. striatula*, which is hardy for Will Giles in Norwich, and which I have found very easy to raise from seed.

They helpfully give a zonal rating for the plants, which might give some indication of

UK hardiness, although whether the plants will stand the winter wet is a matter for experimentation.

Seeds from home

Closer to home, Thompson & Morgan offer a range of exotics including *Datura inoxia* (listed as *D. meteloides* 'Evening Fragrance') which can be planted in the ground and will overwinter in the warmer counties.

Also on their list is *Brugmansia suaveolens*, which in my view is the only brugmansia worth growing from seed.

Seed-raised plants will naturally grow as single-stemmed

"The potential for moving the exotic movement forward is tremendously exciting, and move forward it must, for we must keep at least one step ahead of being packaged for a TV makeover"

ABOVE: *Aloe variegata*

LEFT: *Brugmansia suaveolens*

BELOW: *Canna indica*

standards which will flower in three to six years. This may sound a long time, but two of my named forms, including *B. suaveolens* 'Myles Challis', were grown from seed.

There is still a lot of confusion about brugmansia and datura in the seed catalogues, and you should be aware that, if it's purple, or will flower in six months, it's a datura. Moreover, the double form *B. x candida* 'Knightii', does not come true from seed.

Another member of the Solanaceae offered by T&M is *Iochroma australe* (listed as *Acnistus australe*) which is the only reliably hardy iochroma, eventually growing to a large shrub with either blue or white flowers. Seed packets usually contain both forms.

This does not seem to have been a particularly good year for ipomoea, although I. 'Star of Yalta', also offered by T&M, has been an exception. Whereas 'Star of Yalta' is purple with a pronounced red star, their new cultivar 'Milky Way' is white with a red star.

Chiltern Seeds, also based in the UK, produce an extensive catalogue, including many Australasian plants, with over 60 species of eucalyptus, not all of them hardy. These trees are easy to raise from seed, and it is preferable to do this, as, ideally, they should be planted in the ground when 23cm (9in) tall; this allows them to develop an adequately stabilising root system.

Chiltern also offer something which is very much a plant of the moment – *Musa sikkimensis* (listed as *M. hookeri*). This banana, likely to prove as hardy as *M. basjoo*, has thicker, and hence more wind-resistant, leaves.

Being different

I suspect that one of the reasons I became interested in growing plants from seed is that I don't like to have the same plants as everybody else. Rather, I prefer to have plants in my garden that visitors have never seen before, or that would-be players of Competitive Botany get hopelessly wrong.

With the growing popularisation of exotics by television pundits, trachycarpus and tree ferns are cropping up everywhere, often in the most inappropriate settings. So with a pioneering spirit that is often typical of exoticists, I am getting the urge to find new plants for use in the exotic garden.

This involves a lot of research, much trial and error, heartache, frustration and rude words. But the potential for moving the exotic movement forward is tremendously exciting. And move forward it must, for we have to keep at least one step ahead of being packaged for a TV makeover. And growing new plants from seed is one way we can do this.

Suppliers

■ **Silverhill Seeds**, PO Box 53108, Kenilworth, 7745 Cape Town, South Africa, tel +27 21 762 4245, email rachel@silverhillseeds.co.za, website www.silverhillseeds.co.za

■ **Thompson&Morgan (UK) Ltd**, Poplar Lane, Ipswich, Suffolk, IP8 3BU, tel 01473 680199

■ **Chiltern Seeds**, Bortree Stile, Ulverston, Cumbria, LA12 7PB, tel 01229 581137, email info@chilternseeds.co.uk, website www.chilternseeds.co.uk

■ **B&T World Seeds**, Paguignan, 34210 Olonzac, France, tel 00 33 4 68 91 29 63, email B_and_T_World_Seeds@compuserve.com, website http://b and-t-world-seeds.com/

Succulents
for a sunny conservatory

Shirley-Anne Bell says succulents will leave you more time to enjoy your garden room

Many of us dream of a conservatory full of lush plants, but, sadly, a sunny conservatory can actually be a difficult environment for some plants because providing sufficient watering and ventilation isn't always easy.

The result is that you may find that you spend more time caring for your conservatory than sitting in it and enjoying it.

So try a succulent conservatory instead: there are no delicate leaves to wilt or droop!

Succulence in plants is an adaptation to drought. Cacti, the best known of the succulent plants, have adapted so that their shape has become simplified to a water-storing sphere or column, covered in thick spines

for protection from the heat.

The so-called 'other succulents', e.g. anything other than cacti, have a variety of protective stratagems. In some, their stems have thickened, in others, their roots have swollen, or their leaves have adapted by becoming fleshy, glossy or covered in a grey, sun-deflecting, bloom.

As a result, these plants are

"Lithops are almost completely camouflaged when planted up amongst pebbles and small stones"

ABOVE: Assorted lithops (living stones)

ABOVE: *Rebutia xanthocarpa*

LEFT: Mixed agave bed

RIGHT: *Cleistocactus straussii*

perfect for a sunny conservatory, offering a wonderful variety of shape, size and form, from shrubby to angular, from columns to rosettes, and including trailing forms.

With their brilliant colour palette of pinks, blues, lilacs, yellows, and silver as well as every shade of green, they offer all-the-year-round interest.

For a well-filled look you will need to choose a variety of plants, with a backdrop of clambering and hanging plants and some larger specimens for emphasis.

Smaller plants

In the foreground you can feature smaller plants that earn their keep because of their flowers, their looks or curiosity value,

perhaps arranged in a collection of interesting containers.

Rhipsalis, or mistletoe cacti, form loosely branching spider-like plants with tiny white flowers followed by white berries, and make a wonderful cloudy backdrop to other plants.

The ceropegias, like *Ceropegia woodii*, with their delicate stems, trail attractively, as does *Senecio rowyleyanus*, the string of beads.

Kalanchoes grow vigorously and make resilient hanging-basket choices. Varieties like *K. manginii* and 'Wendy' bear masses of flowers in the late winter or early spring.

For hanging-basket flowers, you can look at the gorgeous, waterlily-like blooms of the epiphyllums (orchid cacti),

ABOVE: *Crassula socialis* in flower

ABOVE: *Crassula* 'Silver Springtime'

ABOVE: *Opuntia violacea*

"Brilliant colour palette of pinks, blues, lilacs, yellows, and silver as well as every shade of green offers all-the-year-round interest"

ABOVE: *Lithops schwantesii* var. *marthae*

and selenicereus (queen of the night).

Epiphyllums and selenicereus have long, pale-green, strap-like leaves which can be used to give background foliage until they amaze you in the spring and summer with their huge bowl-shaped flowers in shades of pink, red, yellow and white.

Selenicereus have a similar form, but their fragrant heads open at night.

Aporocacti and their multitude of hybrid aporocactus/epiphyllum crosses, aporophyllums, have similar dramatic, day-opening, flowers, again in shades of white, pink, red and peach, carried on long, thin, spiny, trailing stems which have

earned them the creepy, and perhaps a little too graphic, common name of rats' tails.

Larger plants

For larger plants for accent planting, look at aeoniums, and all of the agaves, with their variety of spiky, rosette-forming leaves, varying from the thinnest, like *Agave parviflora,* to the thickest, like stripy *Agave americana variegata.*

The larger crassulas, such as *Crassula argentea* (money plant) and its colourful hybrids, 'Hummels's Sunset' and 'Bluebird', make attractive gnarly trees.

Tall columns of cacti make striking additions. Look for cereus, cleistocactus and opuntias. *Cleistocactus straussii* grows into tall columns, covered in soft white hair and bearing strange, almost embryonic, red flowers.

Opuntias will grow their huge, round spiky pads at astonishing rates, and many will flower profusely every summer, with glossy, bright yellow, red or orange flowers.

Although shy to flower, *Opuntia subulata* is one of the best and fastest growing of the opuntias for its form, with dark-green spiky single columns, branching in time. They also make wonderful candelabra if you behead them and allow them to sprout again – you can root the cut part if you keep it in a dry place for a fortnight to callous over.

Flowering cacti

Although flowering cacti are sometimes regarded as mythical beasts there are, in fact, many free-flowering species which will delight with flowers every year in such abundance that the plants are almost invisible.

The basic requirement is a dry, dormant, frost-free period in the winter. Then, rebutias, lobivias, mammillarias and chamaecereus, to name but a few, will spring into bud at the first sign of spring.

The winter-flowering crassulas, like *Crassula socialis* and *Crassula anomala*, are also very appealing, with their columns of overlapping leaves

ABOVE: Left to right, *Echeveria subsessilis, Agave parviflora* and *Echeveria* 'Perle von Nurnberg'

or their loosely-branched, leafy rosette shapes.

They flower profusely with masses of delicate white flowers to lighten the dreariest days of winter. *Crassula* 'Silver Springtime' flowers a little later, this time with raspberry-pink blooms.

Euphorbia milii splendens (crown of thorns), with its spiky stems and attractive flower-like bracts in yellow or red is another worthwhile choice.

Shape and form

The variability of shape and form already mentioned earn a place for many other succulent plants. Some, like *Pelargonium carnosum* and many of the crassulas, make wonderful bonsai-like subjects, looking particularly good

How to care for the plants

These plants will stand strong sunlight and can be watered and fed when you want to.

They are also cheap to look after. Rather than the high temperatures that sub-tropical species require, these plants need only a frost-free environment which can be kept just above freezing in the winter, though many will thrive in an unheated space as long as they are kept dry over winter.

Any John Innes or multi-purpose compost will suit succulents; if you feel you may be tempted to over water, add sharp sand or horticultural grit.

In full growth they appreciate a good soaking once a week, with a feed every two or three weeks, but make sure they dry out completely between waterings. They do not have the natural resistance to fungi and moulds of our native plants, so prolonged moisture is a threat to them.

As autumn draws on, reduce the watering until, in a cool conservatory – around 4-5°C – they are kept absolutely dry from November to March.

In a heated conservatory, all of your plants will need minimal watering over the winter to stop them shrivelling.

From March onwards, increase water very gradually until they are in full growth.

Fortunately, succulent plants are less prone to pests and diseases than many plants. The main pests are mealy bugs – root and stem – which respond to treatment with systemic insecticide.

Red spider mite can be a pest in these dry conditions. You can use a specific mite killer or, strangely, you may find that fungicides are also good red-spider toxins.

Fungal infections are only a problem in damp conditions so, as far as watering goes, you will be pleased to know that you can always take the lazier option – if in doubt, don't!

LEFT: *Calibanus hookeri*

in shallow pottery dishes.

The caudiciforms, such as *Aloinopsis jamessi, Calibanis hookeri*, and the purple-flowered, convolvulus-like ipomoeas, are also good subjects for shallow containers. With their huge, engorged roots, which sit on top of the soil like great fissured rocks, they make

great conversation pieces.

Lithops, also known as living stones or mimicry plants, are almost completely camouflaged when planted up amongst pebbles and small stones.

They come in a variety of mottled grey, green and reddish-brown shades and are great fun for children. They produce striking white and yellow daisy-like flowers in the autumn.

Other good choices are the colourful, flower-like rosettes of the echeverias, aloes, with their thickened, spiky green leaves, often dotted with warts and nodules, and *Cotyledon orbiculata*, with its frosty-grey bloom.

"There are no delicate leaves to wilt or droop"

Which way's

Mike Lewington sorts out the brugmansia from the datura

Brugmansia and datura – both related to potatoes, tomatoes, aubergines and chillis – often cause confusion as to which is which.

In fact the two are different in appearance and life style. Datura are annual, biennial or short-lived perennials, have upward-facing flowers, are self-fertile and produce round spiny fruit whereas brugmansia are shrubby or tree-like, live upwards of 70 years, have flowers angled downwards or fully pendant, are self-sterile, and produce smooth fruit.

Datura

There are two datura species of horticultural merit: *Datura metel* has smaller flowers and green leaves, and is often to be found in the seed catalogues in its double purple and yellow forms; *Datura inoxia* has larger flowers, usually white with a lilac flushing at the mouth, and blue-green leaves, being listed in catalogues as *D. wrightii, D. meteloides* or *D.* 'Evening Fragrance'.

Datura flowers are short-lived, open at night and are mildly fragrant.

Datura are easily raised from seed and will flower around six months from sowing. Sow the seeds in individual 3in pots, 6mm (¹/₄in) deep in John Innes Seed Compost at 20°C; germination occurs from 10 days after sowing. Pot-on in gradually larger pots up to 2 litre size, using John Innes No. 2. Feed with a high potash fertiliser.

In the warmer counties, *Datura inoxia* can be planted into the ground, where it tends to produce a lax plant with rather more leaves than flowers, but is still a fine addition to an exotic planting.

In the ground, the plant produces long, white, fleshy forking roots, which will overwinter while the top growth is cut to the ground. In spring small clusters of leaves will emerge from the crown.

Expect the plant to last about three years, and collect seed from the spiny capsules when fully dried out.

Brugmansia

To help recognise brugmansia, *see panel for varieties*, look at the calyx (sepal) – the green covering that protects the flower bud – and the corolla teeth – the thin extensions at the mouth of the flower.

In some species the bud bursts out of the end of the calyx so that the tips form a zigzag (toothed) pattern. In others, the calyx splits along one side to form a kind of spathe.

Brugmansia are gross feeders and like a

ABOVE: *Brugmansia aurea* 'Golden Queen'

rich diet. Pot them into John Innes No. 3 with a sustained-release fertiliser incorporated into the compost. I would also give them a weekly feed with a liquid fertiliser during the summer.

Part of the reason for this belt-and-braces approach is the fact that brugmansia lose water very rapidly in hot weather and require frequent watering, which leaches nutrients out of the compost.

They should not be positioned where they get the full force of the midday sun, as, apart from wilting, the leaves are prone to sun scorch in low humidity.

They will enjoy being planted directly into the ground and can be lifted before winter. This method produces very sizeable specimens indeed.

Brugmansia can be overwintered in frost-free conditions. If kept in a conservatory or heated greenhouse they will continue to flower spasmodically through the winter.

If the plants are being kept in a dormant state, keep the compost on the dry side to avoid rotting at the base. Avoid repotting late in the season, as rotting is less likely to occur in a root-filled pot. Leaves are likely to drop and some die-back may occur.

ABOVE: Double yellow form of *Datura metel*

up?

ABOVE: *Brugmansia suaveolens* 'Myles Challls', a seed-raised plant with particularly large and white flowers, gives jungle freshness to a dark area...

Pruning

Brugmansia flower when a main stem divides and produces growth characterised by short internodes and tiny leaves. Flowers then appear on these branches a month later. Stems do not divide until they are at least 8cm (3in) high.

Thus, by cutting back to the base – as is common – you will lose at least one flush of flowers, because the plant will have to make up the growth. Prune in spring and remove

ABOVE: ... and in full frontal close-up is simply dazzling

Datura inoxia

ABOVE: Lavender-blue hostas provide a gentle foil for brash *Brugmansia x candida* 'Knightii'...

ABOVE: ... but just look at the delicately subtle green markings of this knight in shining white armour!

any die-back on the branches. If you need to reduce the size, do not cut back beyond the fork. For specimens with several stems, cut back one to the base each year, as old stems often look woody and sparse and this treatment progressively revitalises the plant.

New growth resulting from cutting back will produce much larger leaves. Large leaves in brugmansia are juvenile foliage; as the plant grows and ages the leaves become smaller.

Brugmansia being trees and shrubs, the lower leaves will drop off, leaving the stems bare.

Both datura and brugmansia are prone to red spider and whitefly. Red spider attack produces a yellow mottling of the leaves, which eventually curl, brown and drop off. Fine webbing can often be detected in the forks of branches.

If using an insecticidal spray, make sure to treat the underside of the leaves and into the forks of the branches.

Brugmansia are easily raised from seed in the same manner as datura. They do, however, take at least three years to flower from seed.

Tip cuttings, 8 to 10cm (3 to 4in) in length, can be taken in the autumn and given bottom heat. Or take your cue from the South American Indians by taking 2.5cm (1in) stem cuttings and pushing them into some well-drained soil in part shade, when all danger of frost is past. Dig them up in the autumn and pot to overwinter. This method produces large plants quickly.

Who's who of brugmansia

The horticultural trade and, regrettably, many reference books, muddle up the species, cultivars and hybrids of brugmansia, often applying incorrect names. Use this key to work out which is which – incorrect names are listed in brackets:

■ *Brugmansi arborea* (*Datura speciosa, D. cornigera, D. knightii, D. frutescens*) Rare in cultivation as the flowers are only 15cm (6in) as opposed to 20cm (8in) plus for the other species. It is unusual in that it comes only in an unvarying white. It has a snug spathe-like calyx and 2.5cm (1in) corolla teeth that curl back. One of the hardier species, it will withstand some frosting.

■ *Brugmansia aurea* (*Datura affinis, D. pittieri*) The cultivar 'Golden Queen' is common in cultivation and seems to me no different from the species. It has golden-yellow flowers with a light flushing at the mouth which darkens as the flower ages. *B. aurea* also comes in white and orange forms, although these are rare in cultivation. The calyx is toothed and loose and the 20cm fragrant flowers have 5cm (2in) teeth which curve back.

■ *Brugmansia sanguinea* (*Brugmansia bicolor, B. lutea, B. chlorantha, Datura rosei*) Very common in cultivation and easily recognisable because of its tubular flower. The only species which is not fragrant, it is pollinated by hummingbirds, which have a poor sense of smell, whereas the other species are pollinated by sphinx moths. The flower colour is yellow gradua-

ting to red at the mouth, with a toothed calyx that appears slightly inflated. The flowers are around 20cm in length and have very short teeth that do not curl back. A pure yellow form, *B. sanguinea* 'Flava', is occasionally available. This species will withstand some frosting and large specimens are grown in the ground in Cornwall. *B. sanguinea* only flowers in the cooler months, March to April and October to December.

■ *Brugmansia suaveolens* (*Datura gardneri*) While other species are indigenous to Columbia, Ecuador, Northern Peru and Bolivia, this species originates from a small strip of coastal rain forest in Brazil. It has succeded in naturalising through most of the tropical and sub-tropical regions of the world. The white and pink forms of this plant are common in cultivation and the yellow is occasionally available. The 26cm (10in) fragrant flowers are bell-shaped, and the narrow part of the flower extends well beyond the end of the toothed and loose calyx.

■ *Brugmansia versicolor* (*Datura mollis*) This species is rare in cultivation and plants so named are often a pink form of *B. suaveolens*. Flowers are white, peach-apricot or pink and very large indeed, ranging from

ABOVE: *Brugmansia suaveolens'* pink form is like a blush of pleasure...

"Brugmansia can be overwintered in frost-free conditions"

ABOVE: ... While its yellow form casts a vibrant glow of sunshine

33 to 51cm (12 to 20in). They are fragrant, fully pendant, with 5cm corolla teeth. The calyx is spathe-like and the narrow part of the flower tube extends well beyond its tip.

■ *Brugmansia x candida* (*B. candida*, *B. arborea*, *B. cornigera*) A naturally occurring hybrid of *B. aurea* and *B. versicolor*, with white, fragrant flowers, 20 to 33cm (8 to12in) and fully pendant, with the close-fitting, spathe-like calyx fully enclosing the narrow part of the flower, and 5cm recurving corolla teeth. *B. x candida* is rare in cultivation, but the double white cultivar 'Knightii' is very common. It is the only double brugmansia. The other common cultivar, *B. x candida* 'Grand Marnier', has apricot flowers. Both double and apricot forms of *B. x candida* are naturally occurring, and it may well be the case that there is a range of clones lurking under these names in the trade.

■ *Brugmansia x insignis* (*Datura insignis*) A naturally occurring hybrid of *B. suaveolens* and *B.versicolor* which has only ever been collected as isolated clones. Usually pink and rarely white, the flowers are similar in shape to *B. suaveolens*, but are much larger at 30 to 38cm (12 to 15in) with 6cm (2½in) teeth. The calyx is toothed and loose and the narrow part of the flower extends well beyond it. The flower never fully flares and has a heavy, floppy appearance. Pink forms of *B. suaveolens* are often listed under this name, and the size of the flower and teeth is the best guide.

ABOVE: *Brugmansia sanguinea* is the colour of ripe apricots

Don't try these at home

These plants have a reputation for being dangerously poisonous. I would argue that this is overstated. Brugmansia contain the belladonna group of the tropane alkaloids, primarily hyoscine (scopolamine) and are farmed for the extraction of this chemical, which is widely used in the pharmaceutical industry.

Brugmansia are used by the South American shaman to induce hallucinogenic trances, and are not taken as a recreational drug by other Indians.

Brugmansia intoxication causes a restriction of the visual field and constriction of the throat which makes swallowing difficult. The hallucinations are usually unpleasant.

Brugmansia are, however, important in native medicine and are made up into poultices for the relief of rheumatism, smoked for the relief of asthma, taken internally for the relief of stomach convulsions and getting rid of intestinal parasites.

Naturally I do not recommend trying any of these remedies at home!

Flights of fancy

The bird of paradise plant – one of the most familiar plants of the Mediterranean – can be grown successfully in the UK, providing you offer it some glass protection

The bird of paradise plant, *Strelitzia reginae*, in full blooming glory

"**Bringing flowers home from holiday is seldom practical**"

Visitors to the Canary Island of Tenerife may have been tempted to bring back a box of cut blooms of *Strelitzia reginae* – known as the bird of paradise flower and recognised as a symbol of the island.

But it is actually a native of South Africa, which is why its other common name is the South African crane flower. Fields of plants are cultivated for their exotic flowers, which are long-stemmed with boat-like bracts emerging from the colourful orange and blue flowers. In their natural habitat they are grown with ample space around them, and that, combined with continuous bright sunlight, ensures that plants will produce flowers in reasonable time, which makes these plants an economical crop to manage.

Fully pot-grown strelitzias grow to a maximum height of just over 1m (3ft), and produce a considerable number of long strap-like leaves.

In the conservatory they will do best in full sun and should be freely watered during the spring and summer, giving less in the autumn and very little over the winter period.

Plants can be fed during the growing months; however it is not wise to be over-generous with either feeding or potting on as plants will often produce more flowers if

RIGHT: *Strelitzia reginae* produces a sticky nectar around the flower heads

they are well rooted in their containers and a touch neglected.

How long it will be before seed-grown plants come into flower is a question frequently asked: the answer is about 8-10 years and, unfortunately, the flowers of UK-grown seed-sown plants are frequently inferior to those growing in warmer, sunnier climes outdoors.

If you fancy having a go at growing from seed, sow in the spring in conditions where the temperature does not fall below 20°C, where they should not be difficult to germinate.

When large enough to handle, the seedlings should be transferred to small pots filled with a standard potting mixture. Ensure that plants have ample sunlight and moisture while

they are actively growing in the spring and summer months.

The alternative method of propagation is to remove suckers from around the base of the plant, in spring, and to pot these individually.

It is often said that strelitzias can also be increased by division, but this could be a daunting task and a traumatic experience for the plant: as mature plants they have many solid roots, making separation extremely difficult. It may be possible with younger plants however.

Strelitzia reginae 'Humilis' produces similar flowers, but is slightly dwarfer than straight *S. reginae*, while *S. r.* 'Kirstenbosch Gold' has blooms that are of a much richer gold.

Strelitzia nicolai is an alternative species to grow, with white and pale-blue flowers in boat-shaped bracts.

In its native home it can even reach 8m (25ft) in height, so be warned! *S. alba* is similar, but with all-white flowers, and is slightly smaller at 5m (16ft) when fully mature.

Strelitzia nicolai produces white flowers, but is even more tender than straight *S. reginae*

Strelitzia juncae offers attractive pink/purple flowers (not commonly available in the UK)

The light orange petals of *S. reginae ovarae*

Hybridists are working on new colour forms of straight *S. reginae*, and have come up with this egg-yolk colour

Going potty

■ In the UK these plants can be left on a sunny patio throughout July and August, but otherwise they must be kept under glass. They require a sunny spot, and should be watered daily. Remove withering leaves at their base. *Strelitzia nicolai* is tolerant of shady conditions.

Overwintering: Greenhouse or conservatory, but plants will survive in a cold but frost-free shed or garage.

PLANT PROFILES

'Ardens', the rosy-purple double hibiscus

Hit it with

**Colourful and reliable, hibiscus are hardy enough to bring an exotic touch to your garden.
Graham Clarke chooses some of the best and advises on how to achieve the best from them**

Planning a holiday this year? If you're feeling flush I can recommend Hawaii – you'll enjoy the crash of the waves, the tanned surfers and the stunning scenery. More romantically, there is the sub-tropical moonlight, the seductive rhythm of the hula and the garland-clad beauties with hibiscus blooms placed delicately behind their left ears.

The very name hibiscus conjures an image of lush and gloriously exotic plants, of rainforests and steaming heat. In reality, this is only partly true, and hibiscus are plants that can grace both our British gardens – except those in the coldest parts of the country – and our centrally-heated homes.

Hibiscus is a genus of around 200 plants, and belongs in the same family as abutilons, hollyhocks and mallows (lavatera, malva and sidalcea). They all have the same readily recognisable and generally spectactular trumpet-shaped flowers in numerous shades. Many are charac-terised by what botanists call 'exerted styles' – they protrude a long way beyond the petals, so adding to the exotic appearance.

Hardy hibiscus

Hibiscus syriacus is the form which is hardy enough to grow in the UK; it will tolerate temperatures down to about -15°C, although flower buds may be damaged by late frosts.

Common names for these plants vary, among them being 'tree hollyhocks' and 'flower-of-an-hour'. Although *H. syriacus* has been cultivated in British gardens since the 16th century, its origin isn't known – almost certainly not Syria, however.

The bad news is that the showy trumpet-shaped flowers in red, pink, blue or white each last for just a couple of days. But the good news is that they are produced consistently over a fairly long period – from late summer and well into autumn – just when everything else outside seems to be packing up for the year. The even better news is that some rather

ABOVE: Double hibiscus, like 'Duc de Brabant', are extremely popular

RIGHT: One of the purest of whites –'Diana'

hibiscus

appealing autumn colour can also be had from the attractively serrated leaves.

Hardy hibiscus grow best in full sun – which makes them even hardier – but they will tolerate light shade. They really must have a light, rich, free-draining soil and, if happy where they are, should eventually reach about 2m (6ft 6) in height and spread.

Flowers cluster at the tips of current-year shoots, and pruning is not normally recommended, although on mature plants the previous season's

'Hamabo' – pale pink flowers with crimson centres

ABOVE: Typical hibiscus flowers from the excellent 'Russian Violet'

growth may be shortened by up to half to encourage a bushy habit.

There are now many excellent varieties, but in my experience these are some of the best:

'Ardens', pale rose-purple with maroon blotches; double

'Diana', pure white flowers with crimped edges

'Dorothy Crane', large white single blooms with a feathered red centre

'Duc de Brabant', deep rose-purple; double

'Hamabo', pale pink flowers with crimson centres

'Helene', double white with dramatic red and pink markings

'Meehani', low growing with lavender flowers and leaves with a yellow margin

'Oiseau Bleu' (also called 'Bluebird'), violet-blue flowers with darker centres

'Pink Giant', pink flowers with deep red centres

'Red Heart', white flowers with deep red centres

'Russian Violet', bright lilac-pink flowers with deep red centres

'William R. Smith', large white; single

'Woodbridge', carmine-pink flowers with deep crimson centres

The indoor options

Hibiscus rosa-sinensis, despite its name – meaning rose of China – occurs throughout the warmer parts of the world but did probably originate somewhere in tropical Asia.

In its natural habitat it is a shrub or even a small tree. In the UK it is a shrubby house plant, often treated by commercial growers with a dwarfing agent to keep it compact.

The flowers are generally much larger and more dramatic than the hardy species. The single, red-flowered varieties are the most frequently seen, but there are dozens of cultivated forms, some of which are truly spectacular.

Reds, oranges, salmon-pink, yellows and white-flowered types exist, with a wide range of doubling, and there are some with wonderfully frilled petals.

Whereas indoor hibiscus are frequently seen for sale in garden centres, your choice of

ABOVE: 'Helene' is one of the most dramatic of all hibiscus flowers

ABOVE: The large, white, single 'William R. Smith'

varieties will depend on what is available at the time, but those to watch out for include:

'Cooperi', single, scarlet flowers with cream and pink variegated foliage

'Full Moon', lemon yellow, double, freely produced

'Koeniger', yellow, double-flowered

'Weekend', saucer-sized flowers of rich orange

Best conditions for indoor hibiscus are:

■ Bright light with some direct sun

■ Normal room temperature in the growing season; allow to rest at 13°C during the winter

■ Keeping the compost thoroughly moist at all times during active growth; during winter allow it to dry out between waterings

■ Misting the foliage frequently

■ Feeding with tomato fertiliser

ABOVE: 'Woodbridge' is one of the best selling varieties

ABOVE: The feathered red centre to each bloom is the main feature of 'Dorothy Crane'

ABOVE: 'Weekend' produces flowers the size of saucers

every two weeks in summer
■ Trying not to move the plant when in bud; buds drop off easily!

Hibiscus propagation

Propagating hibiscus is fairly easy and by one of two methods: semi-ripe cuttings and layering.
Cuttings During summer, pull off current-year side shoots and shorten the heel of bark to within 6mm (¼in) of the base. Cut back the unripe tip to just above a leaf to produce a 7-10cm (3-4in) cutting. Insert it in a pot of gritty compost and strike it in a propagator heated to around 18°C. Roots form slowly.
Layering Select a young, low-growing stem and make a sloping cut midway through it,

into the middle of a joint. Wedge open the cut with grit, dust it with rooting hormone and peg it into a compost mixture of equal parts sharp sand and topsoil. Water it in and cover the buried portion with a brick or large, flat stone to keep soil moist and encourage roots to form. This should take a couple of months.

Top 7 tips for very best effect

● **When buying a hibiscus, don't fall for a big one; try to find a small but vigorous, well-budded specimen**

● Don't worry if the individual blooms only last a few days. This is perfectly normal and more will quickly follow

● **Leave any major pruning until after flowering, and then only prune to retain shape and keep the plant tidy**

● Aphids sometimes attack the young foliage, especially of indoor hibiscus, but these plants readily accept treatment with contact insecticides

● **Once established, the hardy hibiscus flower well on fairly poor soils, although growth may be on the slow side. Unlike their tender counterparts, which like rich** living, if the hardies are fed frequently they tend to produce leaves at the expense of flowers

● A handsome alternative to *H. syriacus* is *H. sinosyriacus*. It hails from China and is slightly more spreading. It was introduced in the 1930s by the Hillier nursery family. Look for: '**Lilac Queen**', single lilac flowers each with a scarlet 'eye', and '**Ruby Glow**', single, white with a reddish middle

● **Create a pleasing feature by growing a silver-leaved artemisia next to your hibiscus. Combined with the red, pink, blue or white-flowered hibiscus, the effect will be stunning. Also, you'll find yourself brushing your hands over the silver artemisia to savour the strongly aromatic foliage.**

ABOVE: *Cordyline indivisa*

PUNKS on a STICK

Peter Reid is a self-confessed, fully paid-up member of the Tufty Club for cordyline fanciers

Now I grant you, cordylines have a bit of an image problem. They're kind of the Ikea of plants... undeniably attractive, undoubtedly good value, but – I'm sorry – rather common.

You certainly can't move for cordylines on the south coast, and London is Cordyline City,

where they seem to be flavour of the month for corporate window boxes. Familiarity, as so often, breeds contempt, so you have to ask yourself the question: do you really have room for a cordyline in your exotic garden? After all, who wants a plant that's going to lower the tone?

A year ago I'd have agreed. Then I thought hey, lighten up. Exotic gardening's meant to be fun and cordylines are plants that really know how to party. I mean, how many other plants can you think of that look like a punk hair-do on a stick?

They're also lovely movers. In the wind, their tough, rigid

leaves shiver with tension like a long-term caffeine abuser. And though cordylines might be the poor relation to proper palms, at least they don't stand on ceremony when it comes to growing. Cordylines are the boy-racers of the border. Some even have go-faster stripes.

But, for my money, the really

ABOVE: The green goddess – the aptly named *Cordyline kaspar*

cool thing about cordylines is that they come in a beguiling range of colours. If you're scratching around for foliage to create a striking colour association that comes complete with an exotically tropical twist, chances are a cordyline will fit the bill.

So forget planting them in pots and window boxes or marooning them in the middle of a lawn, the border is where your cordylines really belong.

How they grow
Cordyline australis and *C. indivisa* at first look like a fountain of leaves growing at ground level, but develop a single woody trunk with the leaves forming a tuft on top. *C. australis* can get to 20 metres (66ft) high – wow! – in the wild, but in the UK eight metres (27ft) is about the maximum. It takes several years before it flowers, after which the trunk will branch, giving you several tufts of foliage. If it's cut to the

ground by a vicious winter it usually resprouts, sending up two, three or more trunks to give an attractive multi-stemmed effect when the new trunks form. *C. indivisa* is shorter – from 2-8m (3-27ft) high.

Just to underline the all-round good value of cordylines, their flower panicles have a sweet, heady scent that's like *Lilium regale*.

Even more good news... *Cordyline australis* is much tougher than people used to give it credit for. Severe frosts can damage the leaves; that said, however, this year my garden suffered a 4-day freeze, including a -5°C, and only 'Purple Tower' showed any leaf damage.

To protect the growing point, some people tie up the leaves, but it's probably not a good idea to leave them like this for long periods. A very hard winter can cut *C. australis* to the ground, but it should resprout from the base. I've heard of them regrow-

ing in an Edinburgh garden after a three-week freeze, when the temperature didn't get above -7°C, and which included one night down to a bone-chilling -19°C. *Cordyline indivisa* is even hardier.

Location and choice
Cordyline australis is easy to place. It likes a sunny spot and well-drained soil, with extra watering during dry summers. Strong winds don't bother it. *Cordyline indivisa* isn't so readily pleased, so we asked Paul Spracklin, of Oasis, for advice.

He told us its common name, mountain cabbage tree, is the clue to its cultural problems. In New Zealand it grows up to extremely high altitudes, generally on the western mountain slopes where it's cool and very wet – three metres (10ft) of rainfall a year – but the soil is very free draining. Don't be discouraged, however, for Paul planted five out in 1998 and they're all thriving.

For bobby-dazzling borders...

Young *Cordyline australis*

CLASSIC GREEN

PLAIN GREEN *Cordyline australis* is the original and, many would say, the best. It's a New Zealand native and the Maori used to eat the centres as a green vegetable – which presumably explains its cabbage palm nickname. It isn't actually a palm at all, but what the heck – it looks quite like one. Being standard-issue green, *C. australis* shouldn't offend even the most conservative gardener, while its long, narrow leaves look deliciously exotic. Both young and mature plants are a pretty well indispensable ingredient to cook up a Mediterranean flavour, and it's a good substitute for people whose pockets don't run to decent-sized palms. Small specimens, with their convincing imitation of fibre-optic lamps, look a bit out of place in tropical planting schemes, but they come into their own once the trunks start forming.

STRIPY

THERE'S SOMETHING irrepressible about *Cordyline australis* 'Torbay Dazzler'. Even its name is seductive, suggesting endless sun-soaked days at English seaside resorts. And those vivid cream-and-green stripes do rather put one in mind of a shredded deck chair. As cheery and cheeky as a daffodil in March, 'Torbay Dazzler' must also be a serious contender for the Most Exuberantly Variegated Plant title. Its vibrant colouring is certainly guaranteed to draw the eye, so for my taste it's a bit raucous for the Mediterranean garden – more Viva España than Julio Inglesias. It's probably more at home in the tropical border as a foil to all those big green banana, canna and ginger lily leaves which can get a bit samey without some contrast foliage to lift them. Fans of variegation will presumably have to snap one up regardless.

Cordyline banksii

PURPLE PATCH

THE LEAVES of *Cordyline australis* 'Purple Tower' purport to be purple. They're actually closer to the colour of aged red wine, making this a strangely compelling plant for those whom exotic gardening has driven to drink. This gives the plant a sombre look which

LEFT: *Cordyline* 'Purple Tower'

reminds me of the plumes on Victorian horse-drawn hearses. This isn't necessarily a bad thing – try using it to evoke a contemplative mood in a tranquil part of the garden. Like all the coloured forms of *C. australis*, 'Purple Tower' is a magnificent plant for contrasting with other foliage. For maximum contrast in colour and shape, try it beside the lime-green paddles of a *Musa basjoo* banana.

I've gone for something subtler, combining it with the deeply-cut silver foliage of a globe artichoke against a backdrop of large, green-grey *Magnolia delavayi* leaves.

SOME PEOPLE might baulk at a pink pom-pom poking out of their border. Not me. A plant that makes one think of cheerleaders, bubble gum and Elvis-Sings-Vegas is a must-have. Besides, there's nothing else in nature quite like *Cordyline australis* 'Pink Stripe'. I planted one last autumn and I'm on the edge of my seat waiting for the effect when it reaches 3m (9ft 6in) or more. 'Pink Stripe' is a cordyline that's begging to be used in challenging colour combinations. For something startling, try it next to the dark brown foliage of a smoke tree – *Cotinus coggygria* 'Grace' has superior colouring to the more common 'Royal Purple'. Or for a rather more cool effect, a silver foliage background – provided by, say, a cardoon – will emphasise the leaves' faint light brown stripes.

LEFT: Mature *Cordyline australis* in flower

RAVISHINGLY EXOTIC

UNLIKE THE other cordylines shown here, *Cordyline indivisa* isn't a form of *C. australis*, but a species in its own right. It's also one of the most ravishingly exotic plants you can grow outside in the UK. Its leaves, which can get up to two metres (6ft 4in) long, are broader than those of *C. australis* and look generally more relaxed. They're a soft, dusty green with a fine orange central stripe running down their length. *C. indivisa* is as rare as it is choice – with good reason. It can be as difficult to keep alive as young love, *see main text*. It's also a pig to propagate. So if you see one offered for sale, grab it. Otherwise, there's one at Abbotsbury garden in Dorset, another at Ventnor Botanical Gardens on the Isle of Wight, and several at Wakehurst Place in Sussex that are worth visiting.

RIGHT: Structure and mass – *Cordyline indivisa* cannot obscure the colourful form of *Geranium madareuse*

The different coloured varieties of *C. australis* shown in this feature give only a taste of what is available. Visit almost any good garden centre and the odds are you'll find several others to choose from, with more being added all the time.

There are also other varieties of cordyline you could try, although they're probably only for exotics' fanatics because they're not reliably hardy.

In order of hardiness, Paul Spracklin suggests:-

■ *Cordyline banksii* (the forest cabbage tree) – this grows in forest clearings in New Zealand's north island and the top of the south island, from sea level to around 1000 metres (3,200ft); it's exotic looking, with broadly sword-shaped arching leaves that are substantially longer and wider than those of *C. australis*, and which rise in a distinctive spiral formation – Wakehurst Place, Sussex has a couple of specimens.

■ *Cordyline kaspar* (the Three Kings cabbage tree) – is said to be hardy to -8°C, but this is debatable; with its slightly broader but shorter leaves, it looks like a squatter and stubbier *C. australis* – a few plants are apparently thriving in milder UK gardens.

■ *Cordyline baueri* – is very similar to *C. kaspar*, but even less hardy; I've heard of one growing in Dublin.

Propagation

Cordyline australis and *C. indivisa* can be propagated from seed in spring under glass at 16°-18°C. That said, *C. australis* plants are widely available and inexpensive. *C. indivisa* is very difficult to grow from seed because it has a tendency to rot at ground level – hence its rarity.

So all you have to do now is decide on colour, *see panel...*

■ Oasis Garden Design and Hardy Exotic Plant Sales can be contacted on their website at www.oasis-design.co.uk

True to phorm

Holder of one of the national collections of phormiums, **Christopher Holliday** reveals the secrets of these striking plants

The generous flowers of *Phormium cookianum* make a lovely display in early summer

"The large strap-like leaves provide the exotic gardener with a tough evergreen framework to set the tone"

There should be a place for at least one phormium in every garden. I say this because they are magnificent evergreens that give good contrast and colour variegations in the garden. They soon become focal points as they mature, so the trick is to find ones that suit the space you have available. Once they have reached their full height, which on a P. tenax will be 2m (6½ft) or more, it is not feasible to chop the tops off without ruining the look of the plant, so you need to bear that in mind. The large strap-like leaves provide the exotic gardener with a tough evergreen framework to set the tone, and will offer a good skeletal base on which you can add less hardy exotics. In a western seaboard garden like mine in Grange-over-Sands in Cumbria, they are in their element – they enjoy the mild maritime climate and appreciate the high rainfall of 109cm (43in) per annum.

Species

There are two species of phormium – P. tenax which can reach 2 or 3m (6½ – 10ft) with startling upright leaves, and P. cookianum which will make well over a metre but with a more lax habit. Both will spread to at least a metre in width. In New Zealand, P. tenax flourishes near water, whereas the smaller P. cookianum grows on hillsides. This contrast between upright and arching leaves is the main difference, as the colour variegations are available in both species.

Uses

P. tenax cultivars make good focal point plants and P.

ABOVE: *Phormium tenax 'Purpureum'* make a bold statement in a border

cookianum looks effective when planted in drifts of three upwards. I have a bank of the reliable P. cookianum ssp. hookeri 'Tricolor' made up of seven plants which looks like a great rolling wave. The green and cream striped leaves edged with a red stripe for extra sizzle seem completely impervious to the weather and they are generous with their flowering stems which emerge in May. The back of the border is filled with P. tenax 'Purpureum' and 'Variegatum' cultivars which add height and solidity. The variegated plants complement 'Tricolor', and the 'Purpureum' varieties make a good dark foil.

I am particularly keen on the purple forms and have planted two islands of three in a flat slate terrace in my garden overlooking Morecambe Bay to the south. As the terrace is reached via a steep path, the dark erect leaves are silhouetted, and really enhance the view which is three-quarters sky and one quarter estuary. Phormiums do not like wind but although these are in an exposed spot there are hardly any shredded leaves.

When buying the purple forms, seek out the darkest types as some of them can take on a muddy chocolate look in maturity. There is a very moody-looking black one in the form of 'Platt's Black'.

Tenax

Most of the tenax forms will reach 2 to 3m (6½ – 10ft) in a decade, but if you find the idea of this somewhat intimidating there is a dwarf tenax called

'Bronze Baby' which grows to no more than a metre high. If you have a large garden try the biggest tenax, 'Goliath' which is staggeringly huge and will easily reach 3m (10ft) – not for the faint-hearted though. 'Maori Chief' is a pink and red striped form with bronze leaves which, if planted with the sun behind, becomes translucent. The pink forms are not as hardy as the other cultivars so need a more sheltered location.

Cookianum

Of the cookianum forms, in addition to 'Tricolor' there is 'Cream Delight' which is pale cream with dark green stripes. Found as a sport of 'Tricolor' it is almost as vigorous and the pale leaves illuminate the surroundings wherever it is planted. Another favourite, if you are looking for lightness of touch, is 'Yellow Wave' that has golden leaves with thin green stripes. A bank of these reflect the light at dusk, and lift the spirit even on the most cheerless day. The only drawback is its tendency to form rust spots, caused by damp weather. There is not a great deal you can do about this bar removing the most heavily affected foliage, but it is still worth persevering with them.

These three phormiums will all reach a metre high and will

grow wider than this because of their spreading, arching leaves. Some dwarf forms are ideal if you're tight on space – 'Surfer' comes in green and bronze forms reaching 50cm (20in) in height. 'Jack Spratt' is also miniature with twisted bronze variegated leaves.

Care

Phormiums are best planted in spring in well-drained soil in an open, sunny position. They benefit from lots of moisture in summer but do not want to be waterlogged in winter. They favour a protected position if available – a wall will help them withstand winds and offer some protection in freezing conditions. I would add plenty of compost when planting, to retain moisture, and then mulch with bark or gravel. They will cope with dry weather in their first season, but will grow faster with plenty of water if you can give it. I have found they appreciate water to such an extent that I do not feed them any more now they are established.

Once established, phormiums are reliably low-maintenance and drought-tolerant. I cut off any scruffy-looking dead leaves

BELOW: Height and solidity are the key to *Phormium tenax* 'Variegata'

Phormium tenax 'Maori Chief' has bronze leaves that become translucent with the sun behind them

"I think the point of enjoying evergreen exotic plants is to see them all winter"

in late winter to clean up for the new season. If you do get shredded leaves at the end of the winter you could trim off the split ends on the diagonal. The old leaves die anyway and can be removed at the base to tidy the plant up in spring when these become more noticeable.

Flowers

If they get enough sun, phormiums should reward you with flowers after 3 to 5 years. The most stimulating aspect of phormiums in flower is the height of the stems which stretch out to a maximum of 2m (6½ft) on *P. tenax* and slightly less on *P. cookianum*.

The flowers themselves are small and insignificant, attracting pollinating birds in the wild. The seed-pods are much more eye-catching and last for months. The cookianum seed-pods hang like mahogany-brown runner beans before eventually fading to a silvery transparent sheath. The stems will last indefinitely and on some plants I leave them on for them to bulk out the plant with new stems the following year.

Companions

Once you have introduced one of these bold plants into your garden you may wonder what

best to place with it. Such extrovert foliage calls for something with equal weight, or a complete contrast. The sword-like leaves look more telling when thrusting up between leathery *Fatsia japonica* or the tender *Ricinus communis* in summer. Virtually anything exotic makes a good companion – go wild with bananas, cannas, and hedychiums. If you want a tree, choose *Paulownia tomentosa* and create jungly foliage by cutting it back hard in the spring. Perennial *Melianthus major* with its sharply serrated glaucous foliage works well against purple leaves.

Silvery, Mediterranean fluffy plants such as *Ballota pseudodictammus*, *Artemisia* 'Powis Castle', and *Helichrysum italicum* rest the eye, and the green santolinas or coloured sages create low mounds which are also useful. I find that all types of cistus are good with their fuzzy shape, invariably matt foliage and sun-loving flowers.

It also makes sense to use other New Zealand plants. For a different shape and form look no further than corokias with their tiny platinum leaves and contorted stems. Pittosporums work well with their small leaves and their variety of leaf colour can be used to echo the phormiums. The jet-black 'Tom

Thumb' or the crinkly cream variegated 'Irene Patterson' are ideal. If you hanker after a minimalist approach you could plant a trio of phormiums near a boulder and place a Japanese maple in the background.

Planting time

Now is an excellent time to start planting phormiums so that they can have a full season in which to settle in. Established plants should be hardy to -12°C as long as they are not waterlogged. New plants may need extra mulching. As I live in a mild area on the west coast of the UK I have never protected my phormiums further than mulching them. I think the point of enjoying evergreen exotic plants is to see them all winter. This policy has worked in my garden. In 12 years I have only been caught out once with a freak snow fall of 30cm (12in) which snapped several leaves in half. However, this was the worst snow for 50 years so I feel safe for a while longer.

Containers

Phormiums make good container plants with their sword-like leaves rising abruptly and looking very effective – but they do grow fast in containers so I would recommend re-potting every other year. A congested plant will not only be virtually impossible to remove, but will lose its variegation if starved in a pot. Remember that *P. tenax* will become top-heavy in most containers. Although they are able

ABOVE: *Phormium cookianum* ssp. *hookeri* 'Tricolor' makes an excellent focal point in the garden

ABOVE: The green and cream striped leaves of *Phormium tenax* 'Tricolor'

to cope with freezing conditions in the ground, they are more susceptible to frost damage in a container.

Propagation

Sow seed at 13°-18°C (55°-64°F) in spring. Also divide in spring. This should only be done with a mature specimen. Try and slice as deeply as possible to extricate as much root with the division, leaving the main plant in the ground undisturbed. Unfortunately the foliage far outweighs the amount of root, so keep well-watered. Prune dying leaves to the ground as the new plant will not be able to support all its leaves. New leaves will soon rejuvenate from the centre.

Only for the brave – *Phormium tenax* 'Goliath'

Acacia dealbata

The fluffy yellow flowers of *Acacia dealbata* (mimosa) evoke the sun-drenched Mediterranean, but Freda Cox says this apparently benign tree has a darker past

Anyone who has visited the Riviera in springtime will recall the glorious mimosas which edge roadsides, garland hillsides, shower golden blossoms from lush gardens, and perfume the air with their sweet scent. In mid winter sprays of ferny foliage smothered with tiny ball-like yellow flowers appear in florists to remind us that spring is approaching, and bringing memories of warmer, more exotic sun-filled climes.

Mimosas and wattles, the national emblem of Australia, belong to the acacia family, plants that are associated with biblical times, Ancient Egypt and magical charms.

Origins

Acacias come from tropical and warm regions, most species originating from Australia and Tasmania where they grow in desert margins, on dry, stony ground and forest scrub. The plants have adapted well to warmer climate zones such as African and Mediterranean regions.

The name acacia is derived from the Greek 'akis' meaning sharp point, and is also called tassel tree and silver wattle.

The genus comprises around 1000 species of evergreen, semi-evergreen or deciduous trees, shrubs and lianas.

Description

Alternate, bipinnate leaves are sometimes replaced by flat, green shoots or 'phyllodes'. Leaf stipules often develop woody spines that in some species are inhabited by ants. The plant bears racemes, or panicles, of small, many stamened, globular, fluffy flowers which are usually yellow but can be white or red. Tender to semi-hardy, acacias are ecologically important in dry areas of the world, providing sources of wood and fodder as well as ornament.

Cultivation

Some acacias grow in sheltered positions, standing some degrees of frost, but most require greenhouse protection in the UK.

They need space, good light and ventilation, so plant in greenhouse borders, pots or tubs in equal parts of turfy loam and leaf mould with coarse sand.

Repot established plants every two years in March. Propagate from seed in April or

ABOVE: *Acacia dealbata*

FREDA COX

Uses old and new

Old herbals record acacia as treating eye complaints as well as being incorporated into perfumes for love potions. Bark extracts can be used to make brown dyes and in the tanning process. Some species provide drugs and gums.

Acacia senegal (Cape gum or Egyptian thorn), is a small, spiny trees from tropical Africa which produces gum arabic. This can be used to form a protective and soothing coating for inflammations of the urinary, alimentary and respiratory tracts, and for treating sore throats, coughs and typhoid fever.

Acacia was the sacred Shittim wood of the Hebrews, the ancient Semitic people who built the Ark of the Covenant and Sacred Tabernacle. Spines from it formed Christ's Crown of Thorns.

Egyptian legend tells that a human soul inhabited an acacia tree. The tree was felled but as it died so did its owner. He was brought back to life by a drink made from acacia seeds and became Pharaoh of Egypt.

Ancient Greeks believed mimosa to be a metamorphosis of the maiden Cephisa who changed into a tree to escape the lustful embraces of Pan.

Some consider mimosa to be unlucky, and sinners passing mimosa trees reputedly caused the leaves to close in horror.

The plant is also used as magical charms. In India a sprig of mimosa attached to turbans or above beds was said to ward off evil. And in the 14th century troubadours flocked to France to take part in grand competitions in the hope of winning a golden violet for the best song, Spanish jasmine for the finest pastoral and mimosa for the winning ballad.

take summer cuttings of 5-10cm (2-4in), heeled, half-ripe lateral shoots in sandy compost.

Don't prune, but cut back straggling shoots into the old wood after flowering. Misting helps new growth. Water freely throughout spring and summer, moderately in autumn and winter.

Feed liquid manure at fortnightly intervals from May to August.

Acacia is frost hardy to frost tender.

Generally troublefree, acacia can have problems from red spider mite, tortrix caterpillars which eat young shoots, spinning leaves together, and root mealy bug which causes wilting.

Acacia species

A. dealbata (mimosa) grows from 3-8m (10-26ft), and has glaucous green, ferny foliage and racemes of yellow flowers.

A. armata grows from 2-4m (7-15ft), and flowers freely when young.

A. podalyriifolia (Queensland wattle or pearl acacia) has silvery foliage and is good for cutting.

A. pravissima (oven's wattle) grows to 9m (30ft) is quite hardy and is cultivated in California.

A. verticillata (prickly Moses) grows as low shrub or tree to 9m (30ft).

Mimosa pudica (touch me not) comes from tropical America. Its leaves close when touched and its roots are used an an antedote to cobra bites.

"Egyptian legend tells that a human soul inhabited an acacia tree"

Ginger

Etlingera elatior needs cossetting in a hothouse

"In Hawaii the blooms of *Hedychium coronarium* are used for making flower garlands"

group

The fragrant flowering ginger is an easy plant to grow if you follow the rules, suggests Myles Challis

Next to cannas the gingers are the most important flowering plants in the exotic garden, holding their own against strong structures such as palms, bamboo and bananas.

Cannas supply vibrant colour with their flowers, but the gingers are equally striking for their exotic, almost orchid-like blooms which are often wonderfully fragrant.

The ginger family (zingiberaceae), is a large one and contains several genera, but those most suitable for the garden are the hedychiums.

The hedychiums possess canes ranging from 90cm to 180cm (3-6ft) with opposite rows of leaves varying in width according to the species. These plants are topped with flowered spikes which can range in

ABOVE: *Zingiber officinale*

LEFT: *Alpinia zerumbet*

height from 15cm (6in) to over a foot.

In Hawaii the blooms of *Hedychium coronarium* are used for making flower garlands, while root ginger is obtained from *Zingiber officianale* and cardamon from *Elettaria cardamomum*.

Though the above may have their uses, none is really visual enough to use as a garden plant, and there are many more attractive varieties to choose from.

Choosing a ginger

As hardiness varies quite considerably across the species, the first thing to decide before selecting your plant is how you are going to grow it.

Providing they are well mulched in winter and especially in milder areas, a few gingers

KOBAKOBA

ABOVE: *Hedychium x raffillii*

can be grown outside; others can be grown outside for the summer but overwintered under glass. There are a few exceptions which should be treated purely as greenhouse subjects, where winter temperatures should be maintained between 5-10°C.

The common factor with all gingers is their late flowering – usually August – but as exotic gardens in general are still looking good at this time of year, late flowering should not deter you from growing them.

The rules

Despite their exotic appearance gingers are easy plants to grow

BELOW: *Hedychium x 'Elizabeth'*

LYN SPENCER-MILLS

Alpinia purpurata needs a very warm spot

HARRY SMITH COLLECTION

providing you follow a few rules. Water and feed them well in the summer when the plant is still growing, keep them on the dry side in winter and always avoid disturbance to the roots. Finally, if replanting or dividing, always do so around April.

If you want to try growing gingers permanently outside, choose a warm spot such as a south-facing wall. Incorporate some grit, manure and leaf mould into the soil before planting and bury the rhizomes of the plant 10cm (4in) beneath the surface. In winter cover the roots with a thick mulch and a cloche to avoid excessive wetness.

Much like cannas, any gingers planted permanently outdoors will die down completely in winter and will not appear until May the following year, but gingers are not as fast growing as cannas and certainly do not buck up or multiply quite so quickly.

When overwintered under glass the ginger plants will remain evergreen. This may aid the development of the new canes.

The best method of growing ginger plants is in pots or tubs which, in summer, can be sunk

"Gingers are easy plants to grow providing you follow a few rules"

in the ground or put out on the patio, avoiding any disturbance to the roots.

Hedychiums are greedy plants and should be given a liquid feed about once a fortnight. They prefer a position in full sun or light shade.

Dividing

Gingers take some years to form large clumps, but when it becomes necessary to divide them do so around April when they will be starting into growth.

With a cane, remove lengths

ABOVE: *Hedychium spicatum*

BELOW: *Hedychium 'Lemon Sherbet'*

KOBAKOBA

Hedychium forestii

LYN SPENCER-MILLS

LYN SPENCER-MILLS

HARRY SMITH COLLECTION

ABOVE: *Cautleya gracilis*

of rhizome about 15cm (6in) long with a cane which should have established a sufficient root; plant below the surface of the soil in a pot just large enough to accommodate it.

The compost should be kept moist but well drained.

Once potted, place your gingers in a warm greenhouse until they are established – be patient though, new divisions will not flower in the first year but should after that.

Hedychiums look good when accompanied by most hardy exotics, but fare particularly well with bananas. A clump of *Hedychium gardnerianum* planted at the foot of an abyssinian banana (*Ensete ventricosum*) makes for a stunning sight.

Under glass

The varieties best suited to overwintering under glass are among the most spectacular. One of my personal favourites is *Hedychium gardnerianum*, otherwise known as the 'Kahili' ginger.

The 'Kahili' has lush broad leaves mounted on stems 1.83m (6ft) high and is topped by huge 30cm (12in) flower spikes with yellow petals and orange stamens. This particular plant gives off a luscious scent.

Hedychium coronarium is of a slightly smaller stature and has white flowers which are also beautifully fragrant – hence its popularity as a garland flower in Hawaii.

These two species have been crossed to produce *Hedychium*

Hardy varieties

Hedychium forrestii
Grows to about 1.5m (5ft) and has fragrant white flowers which are usually the first to appear

Hedychium densiflorum
Known as 'Assam Orange', this can grow to about 91cm (3ft) with narrow spikes of densely packed dark orange flowers

Hedychium spicatum
Of similar stature to *Hedychium densiflorum* this variety has white scented flowers.

Hedychium coccineum
One of my favourites, 'Tara' rises to about 1.5m (5ft) with large spikes, orange petals and red stamens

Hedychium yunnanense
At around 1.2m (4ft) *Hedychium yunnanense* has scented white flowers with a red and yellow throat

Hedychium greenei
This plant is worthy for its foliage as well as its flowers. The 1.2m (4ft) red stems sport bare deep-green leaves with maroon undersides while the flower spikes are large and deep orange – but sadly have no scent. This ginger needs copious watering or it will not flower, making it an ideal candidate for planting beside the pond.

Cautleya gracilis
Of smaller stature than the others, 'Syn. Spicata' only rises to 76cm (2.5ft). This ginger has yellow flowers with brownish-red bracts.

ABOVE: *Hedychium coronarium*

x *raffillii*; a lovely hybrid growing to about 1.22m (4ft) and sporting flowers of pale orange with red stamens.

Another one of my favourites is *Hedychium flavescens*, a bold plant with large flower spikes, white petals and orange stamens. This particular plant has a delicious fragrance.

The flowers of hedychiums take several days to open fully and, once opened, will only last a few days. As not all of the spikes on a clump open at exactly the same time the flowering period is slightly extended.

New breed

American breeder Tom Wood has produced some lovely cultivars including *Hedychium* x 'Elizabeth' which is unusual for its pink flowers.

Tom's *Hedychium* 'Lemon Sherbet' has waxy yellow petals and orange stamens and a

LEFT: *Hedychium coccineum* 'Tara' gets some tender loving care

Hedychium gardnerianum

KOBAKOBA

sumptuous fragrance while *Hedychium* 'Luna Moth' has white flowers and a powerful perfume.

Other genera of the ginger family are more tropical and are therefore best kept as permanent greenhouse subjects, but some, such as *Alpinia zerumbet*, may well be worth trying outdoors in milder summer climates.

Alpinia zerumbet, the 'shell' ginger, can grow 2-3m (6.6-10ft) high and displays pink flowers; the yellow variegated form, though a beautiful foliage plant, is strictly for the greenhouse.

Alpinia purpurata, a lovely red-flowering ginger commonly seen in the tropics, can be tried in a very warm spot, as can some of the costus species.

The monster of the ginger family is *Etlingera elatior*, the

"The monster of the ginger family is *Etlingera elatior*, the 'torch' ginger – definitely a hothouse plant"

'torch' ginger which requires high temperatures and humidity – definitely a hothouse plant. *Etlingera elatior* produces waxy red cones on 1.2m (4ft) stems while the foliage can soar up to 5.5m (18ft).

If you add some gingers to your exotic garden, I guarantee that when in flower they will amaze your visitors with their exotic blooms and delicious perfume.

Alongside cannas and daturas, gingers create a scene so convincingly tropical that you feel you are anywhere but the cool climate of Britain!

The National Collection of hedychiums is held by Lyn Spencer-Mills in Somerset.

Torchlight
PROGRESSION

Canna foliage can offer nearly as much enjoyment as the flowers (inset). This is C. 'Tropicana'

PICTURES: HARRY SMITH COLLECTION

That Victorian parks' show-off, the canna, makes a big impact in today's exotic gardens, says **Myles Challis**

No exotic garden is complete without these wonderful plants whose lush banana-like leaves and vibrantly coloured flowers stand out like glowing torches amidst the background of rich greenery that the permanent subjects provide.

Although not hardy, cannas are very easy to cultivate – in much the same way as dahlias – and they will tolerate quite rough treatment. As with dahlias, lift the rhizomes for storage in a frost-proof place for the winter, but in very mild areas some may be left in the ground provided they are well mulched. This practice, however, does depend on the variety and the soil conditions in which they are growing as some are less hardy than others.

Cannas had their heyday in Victorian times when they were used for sub-tropical gardening – also widely practised by the parks' departments. Battersea Park was well known for bedding schemes including everything from hostas to Abyssinian bananas as well as cannas.

The beds in which they were grown were often raised, allowing heat obtained from the sun during the day to be stored overnight, and this is no doubt why such good results were achieved, with many cannas often reaching 3-3½m (10-12ft) in height.

"Most of the popular cannas today have quite large 'gladiola'-like flowers"

ABOVE: The golden-yellow flowers of C. 'En Avant' are sprinkled with red dots

LEFT: *Canna Tropicana*

Despite this, however, the formal style of planting in blocks or rows, still practised by the parks today, does not do the plants justice. Cannas, like all exotics, are much better when planted in the informal setting of the sub-tropical garden. It may, however, be that due to their wide use up until today by the parks that some varieties are still in cultivation.

The Victorian nurseries produced hundreds of varieties, most of which, sadly, have disappeared. Nonetheless, there is now a good selection available, some produced by specialist growers who have no doubt become aware of the growing interest in and popularity of these plants.

Cannas, or 'Indian shot' as they are sometimes referred to – a name derived from the hardness of their round black seeds – are mostly native to tropical and subtropical America. Grown outside, they range in height from only a few feet to as much as 3m (10ft) and some grow larger under glass.

The colour and size of the foliage and flowers is also very variable, species tending to have smaller flowers.

Canna choice

Most of the popular cannas today have quite large 'gladiola'-like flowers but one exception is the lovely *Canna iridiflora*, sometimes called *Canna x ehemanii*. This is one

Cultivating cannas

If you buy cannas as rhizomes (roots) the best time to pot them up is late March or early April. If you start them too early they will be drawn (etiolated) due to inadequate light. They should be grown under glass until late May when they can be planted out.

Cannas benefit from being given gentle bottom heat when first potted, but this is not essential. When they are sprouting strongly, by which time they will have formed new roots, they can be moved on to an ordinary bench or staging in the greenhouse or conservatory in a light position.

Any multi-purpose compost will do. They should be started off initially in a temperature of 18-20°C, but when they have sprouted it can be reduced to 15°C. This way you should have strong, stocky plants.

Plant them in groups of at least three or five plants in a sunny position in good moist soil to which some manure has been added, and water well through the growing season.

Cannas can be left in the ground until the foliage is lightly frosted as this does no harm to the roots.

Lift them, shaking off most of the soil, and store in a little peat in a dry frost-proof place. The foliage can be trimmed back when it has withered.

Cannas usually multiply quite well in the growing season, and the roots can be divided every second or third year, which is also beneficial to the plants.

"Cannas usually flower from July onwards and bloom for a couple of months"

ABOVE: *C.* 'Petit Poucet' has dark yellow flowers with a touch of red

RIGHT: Typical orangy-red flowers of *Canna indica*. The lower petals are marked in yellow

of the best, with very large green leaves and small pink flowers on a pendulous spike. It is a strong-growing plant usually reaching 1.8-2.4 (6-8ft) in height.

Canna musifolia also has large leaves, but with dark maroon veining and stems. It is shy to flower but is a magnificent foliage plant often reaching 3m (10ft). Both these two species have long been in cultivation and are often mentioned in Victorian books.

Some of my favourite cannas are the ones with purple or bronze foliage.

Canna 'King Humbert' is one of the best, with deep purple foliage and blood-red flowers but is difficult.

Also hard to obtain is *Canna* 'Australia', with very dark glossy, purple foliage and orange-red flowers.

Easier to find is *Canna* 'Wyoming', with purple leaves with a green feathering and apricot-orange flowers, and *Canna* 'Assaut' with similar

leaves but flowers the colour of *Lobelia cardinalis*.

Another is *Canna* 'Black Knight' with bronze foliage and dark red flowers.

All these varieties grow a good 1.2-1.5m (4-5ft) tall, but *Canna indica* 'Purpurea' with bronze leaves and orangy-red flowers usually tops 1.8m (6ft).

If you prefer shorter-growing varieties, *Canna* 'Firebird' has bright green leaves and large scarlet flowers with a little yellow in the throat. It is a good easy grower at around 1m (3ft).

The same can be said for *Canna* 'King Midas' which for a change has yellow flowers.

Some cannas have spotted flowers, like the distinctive *Canna* 'Mayerbeer' which is golden-yellow with red spots.

At the smallest end of the scale, at only 50cm (2ft), we have *Canna* 'Lucifer' with bi-coloured red and yellow flowers, and *Canna* 'Gnom' with large salmon-pink flowers. Personally I think these very

short varieties look best in pots as they are too small for the border.

Variegated varieties

Probably the most popular of all cannas are the variegated ones. The first to appear is *Canna* 'Striata' syn. *malawiensis*. The acid-yellow striping on a green background is lovely, and the stems are often reddish, the flowers being rich orange.

When *Canna* 'Durban' appeared a few years ago it caused a sensation. Sometimes sold under the name 'Tropicana', it has foliage of stunning colourations:

salmon-pink veining on a dark purple ground. I would have preferred that the mandarin-orange flowers were red or even pink, but despite this it is a wonderful plant and has been the best selling canna so far.

Of more recent introduction (1998) is *Canna* 'Stuttgart' from the USA. This has elegant sea-green foliage with irregular broad white banding, but this variegation is unfortunately very prone to scorching even in semi-shady conditions. This plant, which has small apricot flowers, will certainly never prove as popular as *C.* 'Durban'.

All these variegated kinds

Not many people know this
Arrowroot is obtained from *Canna edulis*. This species has green leaves with small orange/pink flowers

LEFT: *C.* 'Praetoria' has green leaves with striking yellow veins, plum colouring in the stems and large orange flowers

reach a good 1.2-1.5m (4-5ft) or so.

What not many people may realise is that there are some water cannas. Hybrids of *Canna glauca*, these can be grown either as marginals or in pots stood in water or in the border, provided that they are all kept moist. These plants can be recognised by their slender glaucous foliage and delicate flowers. The best, I believe, is *Canna* 'Endeavour', with raspberry-red flowers.

Overwintering

Cannas usually flower from July onwards and bloom for a couple of months. Even when they have finished flowering they still look good standing up to the autumn gales well after many ordinary garden plants have long since withered.

If you live in a mild location such as Devon or Cornwall, or in the micro-climate of a big city, you could try leaving some of your cannas in the ground over winter. As a precaution however I would suggest that you lift half of each kind as insurance in case those left in situ do not survive.

If they do they will not appear until June, but soon make rapid growth, eventually catching up with those brought on under glass. They are most likely to survive in areas where the frost is light and the soil not too heavy or wet, which would rot the tubers.

In the Victorian's Battersea Park plantings some cannas were left in the ground, but because the beds were raised the drainage was good, improving their chances.

With the popularity of exotic gardening increasing at the present rate it looks as though cannas are enjoying a glorious revival. Anyone already smitten by these wonderful plants cannot fail to see how essential the cannas are in adding the finishing touch to an otherwise incomplete picture.

Plant cannas with...

The most important role of cannas in the exotic garden is the provision of flower colour, especially the bright reds. They do, of course, compliment all hardy exotics, but one or two companions in particular make beautiful combinations.

The best of these are the true castor-oil plants, *Ricinus communis*, especially the purple or bronze-leaved kinds such as *R.c. gibsonii* and *R.c.* 'Carmencita'. These are annuals so have to be grown from seed, but they will still reach anything from 1.2-2.5m (4-8ft) in height depending on the summer. Their large star-shaped leaves make a wonderful contrast to the pointed upright leaves of the canna.

Melianthus major, a much-loved foliage plant with serrated glaucous sea-green foliage, looks particularly good with purple-leaved cannas such as 'Assaut' and 'Wyoming'.

The gingers (hedychium), which I shall be writing about in a later issue, again provide contrast in their different leaf form and orchid-like beautifully perfumed flowers.

"Cannas are much better when planted in the informal setting of the sub-tropical garden"

BELOW: Cannas compliment all hardy exotics

Nerine undulata **leans graciously away from the house wall**

Cape

Labelling yourself an 'exoticist' means you have the perfect excuse for growing all manner of weird and wonderful plants from around the globe. Listings in specialist catalogues that include the words 'choice' or 'rare' are enough to put your credit card into instant arrest, and make you fully aware that the decision to buy will probably result in an untimely death somewhere in the depths of winter.

But this needn't always be the case. Just occasionally the perfect antidote to a little late summer jungle fever has probably been right under your nose all the time. It's got some of the lushest blooms you've ever seen, comes from the exotic if arid East Cape of South Africa and has been grown by legions of gardeners for many, many years.

The plant in question is the nerine or diamond lily, and it's one of those amazing autumn flowers that no garden, exotic or not, should be without. The

BELOW: *N. bowdenii* make a rich bed of colour

PICTURES: HARRY SMITH COLLECTION

ABOVE: *N. sarniensis* major

RIGHT: *N. sarniensis*

"Nerines can be propagated in three ways, two are easy and will give instant results, the third is rather slow but nonetheless rewarding"

crusaders

One of our most spectacular autumn bulbs is worth a place in any garden, exotic or not. **Mike Pilcher** extols the virtues of nerines

RHS agree and have awarded it an Award of Garden Merit.

As bulbs go, nerines have star potential written all over them. They're easy to grow, have superb green, strap-shaped leaves, and flower-heads that may carry up to 25 individual blooms. Unusually, the flowers appear first, usually in September and October, and then as they subside the leaves are produced from the bulb below ground.

Although there are 30 different species, their warmer native habitat and preference for dryish, free-draining soil conditions means that most are more suited to the confines of the greenhouse or conservatory in the UK.

UK survivor

However, amongst this South African clan is one, *Nerine bowdenii*, that will survive quite happily outside if planted in a warm and sheltered spot in the garden. At the base of a south or west-facing wall is ideal. Here the bulbs will get the best

of the sunshine and be protected from the worst of the winter wet. They'll also relish the dry conditions that lesser plants would find intolerable.

Given a deep, dry mulch of compost or straw in the winter to protect the bulb from frost and cold, the bulbs will usually come through unscathed and gradually multiply. In five years time you'll be lifting the clumps, dividing, replanting and giving spare bulbs away to gardening friends. As a contrast, or if you're looking for something a

Pests and diseases

Inevitably, something so good has to have a down side, and in the case of nerines it's the fact that they are on the slug and snail menu for this time of year. However, damage is rarely severe and never fatal so good hygiene and a watchful eye should keep things in order.

ABOVE: The simplest propagation method is to lift and divide clumps after flowering

ABOVE: Beautiful *N. bowdenii*

RIGHT: *N. filifolia*

LEFT: Nerine bulb cut for propagation

BELOW: *Nerine alba*

bit more subtle, try *N.b. alba* whose flowers are white or slightly flushed with pink.

Examine the flowerhead of any nerine and you'll see that it's made up of typically 8-12 individual lily-shaped flowers. Look closer and you'll see that the margins of the petals are frilled, often turning back on themselves at the tip. Over-long stamens in the centre of the flower give an almost spidery appearance.

Needless to say the hybridists have been at work, although most of their attention has been directed to the tender species that we either can't grow or are grown commercially for cut-flower production.

Two hybrids of *Nerine bowdenii* worth a mention are 'Mark Fenwick' (also listed as 'Fenwick's Variety') with its pink flowers and darker stems, and the appropriately named 'Pink Triumph'.

On the tender side

For very favoured outdoor locations, the greenhouse, conservatory or generous windowsill, the Guernsey lily (*Nerine sarniensis*) and *N. undulata* are worth a try. These two are only half hardy and will tolerate temperatures down to 0°C but no lower.

The flowers of *N. sarniensis* are a vibrant orange-red with long stamens that appear to burst out of the fairly compact flowerhead. A scarlet-flowered form, called *N.* 'Corusca Major', is grown commercially as a cut flower and lasts well in water – as all nerine flowers do if you can bring

yourself to cut them.

Nerine undulata has fractionally larger individual flowers in a delicate shade of candy pink.

Two species that will thrive in the well-drained conditions afforded by a rock garden or scree are *N. filifolia* and *N. masoniorum*. Still on the tender side, they're perhaps best grown in large pots, plunge bedded and brought into the greenhouse or conservatory for the worst of the winter.

Both have almost grass-like leaves which are replaced as the old ones die so the plant is practically evergreen. With *Nerine filifolia* the flowers are pink to white and typically frilly, *N. masoniorum* has pink flowers that possess a deep red vein down the centre of each petal. Both

"Just occasionally the perfect antidote to a little late summer jungle fever has probably been right under your nose all the time"

will reach a height of no more than 30cm (12in).

Propagation techniques

Nerines can be propagated in three ways, two are easy and will give instant results, the third is rather slow but nonetheless rewarding.

The simplest thing to do is lift and divide clumps after they have flowered in the autumn.

Remembering that as they generally prefer to be left

alone this may affect the subsequent season's flowers but it's nevertheless a chance to retain the younger, more vigorous bulbs, and discard the rest.

Alternatively, if you just want one or two new bulbs you can sometimes remove offsetts from the side of a clump without too much disturbance to the rest of the plants.

The real enthusiast may wish to try sowing some of the soft, fleshy seeds that are produced as the flowers fade.

This requires more than a modicum of patience. Sown fresh, they'll germinate quite easily given a temperature of 16°C. However, it will probably take up to five years for the bulbs to reach maturity and flowering proportions.

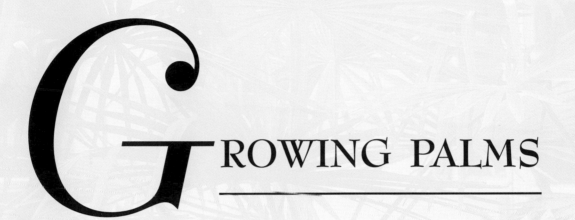

GROWING PALMS

Perfect palm
propagation

Follow the ground rules and you should be able to produce
spectacular palms from seed, says **Martin Gibbons**

ABOVE: What a whopper – the seed of the double coconut can weigh as much as 18kg

ABOVE: The dark colour of coconut peat fibre is ideal because it allows the white sprouting shoots to be easily seen

ABOVE: Mix the seeds with moist peat and place in a clear, labelled and dated plastic bag

ABOVE: Take the seedlings from the bag when the shoot is about 2.5cm long and place in a deep pot

Tricks of the trade

Some growers have their own techniques which are claimed to speed the process or increase the success rate. These include soaking the seeds in acid, scarifying them with a sharp knife or file, providing alternating day and night temperatures, and blowing pure oxygen over them. It must be said, though, that most fresh palm seeds will sprout without these treatments.

A II palms grow from seeds, and some also propagate from suckers. The most familiar palm seeds are those in dates and coconuts, but others include those of the oil palm (*Elaeis guineensis*) – cultivated by the million in the tropics for the production of palm oil used in cooking and soap – and the saw palmetto (*Serenoa repens*) – increasingly used for the treatment and prevention of prostate cancer.

Some seeds, like those of washingtonia – about the size of a match head – are tiny, while others are huge; the seed of the double coconut (*Lodoicea maldivica*) is the largest in the vegetable kingdom and weighs up to 18kg (40lb).

Growing palms from seed is easy and fun, and it is perfectly possible to grow a beautiful palm for home or garden. Following a few rules should make the process easier and less prone to failure.

To germinate successfully most palm seeds need to be fresh, and lack of success can often be traced back to the fact that the seeds were stale. Those from the world's rainforests may be viable for only a week or two; since they grow in permanently wet places, they don't need to wait for rain and can begin to grow immediately. On the other hand, desert palms (such as phoenix, hyphaeno and brahea), may have to wait months or even years for rain so they must last much longer; and washingtonia seeds are said to be still viable after 10 years!

Drupes

Palm seeds are technically drupes – a hard stone inside a fleshy fruit. Plums or peaches are more familiar examples. Sometimes this flesh is reduced to a thin, dry layer, but it is always there. Inside the stone is the seed itself, and the stone is normally planted intact.

ABOVE: Place the seed just below the soil surface, with the shoot exposed

RIGHT: First leaves resemble blades of grass

"The seed of the double coconut is the largest in the vegetable kingdom and weighs up to 18kg"

In the case of the coconut (*Cocos nucifera*) and some others, the seed is hollow and contains a tasty liquid.

As an indication of ripeness, the flesh may well be red, brown or black. Green fruits probably don't contain ripe seeds. Irrespective of fruit colour, however, the endosperm, of which the kernel is largely composed, will always be hard and white.

Ripeness check

Check for ripeness by cutting a few fruits open with a sharp knife; if you can dent the kernel with your thumbnail the seeds are almost certainly not ripe.

With a knife, remove any fruit remaining on the seeds, then wash them in water. The flesh sometimes contains inhibitors which are there to prevent the seed from germinating too soon, so it's important to remove this.

Some flesh can be very fibrous and hard to remove, but a few days' soaking should do the trick. Professional growers may even resort to using a paint mixer on an electric drill to remove this tough coat from a bucketful of seeds. The seed coat itself is very hard and does not suffer in this process.

Palms to grow from seed

Examples of palms that are easily grown from seed are the European fan palm (*Chamaerops humilis*), the Canary Island date palm (*Phoenix canariensis*), the chusan palm (*Trachycarpus fortunei*), and the California cotton or skyduster palm (*Washingtonia species*).

All of these can easily be collected on any holiday to Spain or the south of France. The date palm of commerce (*Phoenix dactylifera*) can readily be grown from seed saved from boxes of dates at Christmas. Somewhat more difficult and erratic to germinate are the butia palm (*Butia capitata*) and the Mexican blue palm (*Brahea armata*), which are nonetheless worth persevering with. They are often to be found in parks and gardens on the Continent.

ABOVE: *Trachycarpus fortunei*

Germination

When the seeds are clean, leave them to soak for a few days, changing the water every day. Then mix them with moist peat and place in a clear, labelled and dated plastic bag. Coconut peat fibre is excellent for this purpose. It is uniformly dark in colour, so the new white sprouting roots can be readily seen. Additionally it is quite light and airy, qualities which may well help the germination process.

As an indication of how moist the compost should be, you should just be able to squeeze a drop or two of moisture from a fistful. Any

"If you can dent the kernel with your thumbnail the seeds are almost certainly not ripe"

more and it is too wet, indicating the addition of some dry peat. Any less, and you should add a little water until the balance is right.

The palm's origin gives a guide as to the temperature at which the seeds will germinate best. Cool-growing palms – trachycarpus, parajubaea, ceroxylon – require no heat at all, so just keep the bag at room

ABOVE: European fan palm (*Chamaerops humilis*)

temperature. More tropical palms do require heat for the seeds to sprout so place in an airing cupboard, on top of a central heating boiler, or perhaps into a purpose-made propagator, or anywhere where the temperature will remain at around 25°C.

Too high a temperature will

prevent the germination process from taking place; too cool and the process will be delayed, perhaps forever. The temperature may fluctuate, and no light is required.

If all goes well, the seeds will germinate in anything from a week or two to a year or two. Most sprout within about 8-12 weeks. Check the bag regularly; you will see the white shoots through the clear plastic.

California cotton or
skyduster palm
(*Washingtonia species*)

Potting up

The seedlings should be removed from the bag when the shoot is about 2.5cm (1in) long, and potted up into a deep pot – yoghurt pots are ideal – using multi-compost. Plant it so that the seed is just below the soil surface, with the shoot exposed.

Place the pot where the light is good, but not in direct sunlight. Water the soil, and aim to keep it uniformly moist thereafter. Never allow it to dry out.

Seedlings make quite slow growth to begin with, but speed up as they get bigger. Pot on as required but don't rush to do it. Most palms' first few leaves are simple, like thick blades of grass, and it may be a couple of years before they begin to develop the familiar fan, or feather shape.

During this time they need a little gentle feeding with any house plant fertiliser, but don't overdo it. Hardy palms may not be big enough to be planted out into the garden for four or five years; don't attempt to do so until the roots fill a 5 or 6in pot.

Martin's tips

If you collect palm seeds while on holiday in exotic places, try to get them from the tree itself; those on the ground may well be predated by insects, or may even be from the previous year's crop.

If purchasing from a seed dealer, enquire as to the seeds' freshness. Check the packing date on the packet: under EU law these days this date must be shown. Don't store the seeds but plant them straight away.

Growing palms from seed may be slow but the process is infinitely satisfying, and one which will give a real feeling of accomplishment.

"To germinate successfully most palm seeds need to be fresh"

Trachycarpus fortunei

Hairy palms

Growing palms outdoors is no longer solely the hair-raising domain of the botanically barmy. Peter Reid picks some tough cookies which really can take on a British winter and still come up grinning

Suddenly, palms are back in business. After being briefly in vogue with the Victorians, they fell out of favour. But now, all of a sudden, they're popping up everywhere, perhaps because of all those foreign holidays we take nowadays. We come back with brave new gardening ideas – as well as a heat rash and streaming cold.

My favourite theory, though, is it's our usual preoccupation – the weather. Whether or not the globe really is getting warmer, we think it is. So planting palms is the gardening equivalent of us all taking off our collective cardy.

Long may it last. Because few plants are quite as glamorous as a palm. Just try imagining a desert island... the mental picture isn't complete without at least one palm tree, is it?

This, perhaps, is the real beauty of palms. They transport us to de luxe hotels on the Côte d'Azur, torrid jungles and languid lagoons. Palms are Bounty commercials. Palms are James Bond films – and you just don't get better than that. And all this can be yours simply by planting one in your garden.

Where you plant it is up to you. Palms make fine specimen plants – my Canary Island date palm (*Phoenix canariensis*) looks a picture in the middle of my lawn. But they work just as well in the border. Their deeply-cut leaves contrast well with the jungly leaves of bananas, cannas and gunneras. Or use them to complement the spikier mood of Mediterranean planting like agaves, cordylines and yuccas.

Whatever you do with your palm, though, one thing's for sure. An exotic garden without a palm is like a Martini without an olive. Perfectly palatable – intoxicating, even – but with the vague, uneasy feeling that something's missing.

TRACHYCARPUS FORTUNEI

Common name: Chusan palm
Place of origin: Himalayas, from Burma to E. China
Hardiness rating: to -15°C
Eventual height: to 10m (30ft) or more

VIRTUALLY WHEREVER you live in the UK, you can grow this palm. That said, try to buy one the size you want – when small, they're so slow they make snail racing look like a compelling spectator sport. The Palm Centre reckons if you water and feed them like mad, they can put on 30cm (1ft) of trunk a year. Mmm. Frost holds no terrors for the Chusan. Wind, however, is its worst nightmare, demolishing the leaves, so pop it somewhere sheltered – or buy *Trachycarpus wagnerianus* which has smaller, tougher leaves. It's happy in full sun or shade, although in sun it develops peculiar yellow flowers that Architectural Plants describes as resembling big yellow haddocks – they can be quite a talking point if you're not a natural conversationalist.

CHAMAEROPS HUMILIS

Common name: Mediterranean fan palm
Place of origin: Europe
Hardiness rating: to -12°C, lower when larger
Eventual height: 2-3m (6-9ft)

ANOTHER frost-busting, easy-to-please palm. If you can't grow this, give up gardening, or move. If wind is a problem, it's a better bet than a Chusan because it's wind – and snow – resistant. And where the Chusan aspires to be tall and elegant – kind of like a hirsute Audrey Hepburn – *Chamaerops humilis* is a stocky, sturdy little bruiser, a sort of bull terrier of the border. It also sends up suckers, so you could end up with a gang of them, which has to be a bit of a bonus. And being Europe's only native palm, it's perfect for conjuring a Mediterranean mood in your garden. It's not fussed whether you plant it in full sun or partial shade, as long as you feed and water it well during the summer – sounds almost human.

SABAL PALMETTO

Common name: Palmetto palm
Place of origin: USA
Hardiness rating: to -12°C
Eventual height: 10-16m (30-50ft)

THIS IS THE state tree of Florida, but it's no Mickey Mouse palm. For a kick-off, it can get very tall, although when it's big it looks wispy rather than weighty. It's a suggestion which came from Shaun Hogan, Director of Collections at Hoyt Arboretum, Oregon where, as well as having a climate rather like our own, the plucky pioneering spirit that made America what it is today lives on in its approach to gardening. Shaun reckons you should be able to grow *Sabal palmetto*, provided you don't live somewhere prone to hard freezes. It's very salt tolerant, so the seaside sounds a good bet. If you can give it good fertile soil, and plenty of feed and water, it should reach a respectable size. But, he warns, it is a slow grower.

JUBAEA CHILENSIS

Common name: Chilean wine palm
Place of origin: Chile
Hardiness rating: to -11°C
Eventual height: big

NO-ONE SEEMS to want to commit to how big this palm gets. Maybe it's because it's such a slow grower that no-one has hung around long enough to find out. There's a 9m (30ft) one in Torquay, so you get the idea. Even its leaves can get to 6m (20ft) long. It's also massively trunked – a bit like having a one-legged elephant standing in your garden. My transatlantic phone call to Shaun Hogan in Oregon revealed that he's seen Californian specimens with trunks 2m (6.5ft) across... lordy. It shrugs off even severe winters once established. Until then, give it protection. Apparently it grows faster in the ground than in a pot, and it wants sun, a south-facing position... and, er, lots of room.

BUTIA CAPITATA

Common name: Butia or jelly palm
Place of origin: Brazil and Uruguay
Hardiness rating: to -10°C, or -12°C when larger
Eventual height: 6m (20ft)

THINK COPACABANA beach. Think Samba. Think *Butia capitata*. Now just think how gob-smackingly gorgeous this palm from Ipanema would look jutting out of one of your borders. *Butia capitata* is one of the hardiest 'feather palms' – which means its leaves look more like long feathers, rather than the fan-shaped leaves of the appropriately named 'fan palms'. The leaves are a bluey-green and strongly curved, giving the crown and thick trunk a compact look, a bit like a dishevelled green cotton bud. Being Brazilian, it's no stranger to high rainfall and, if you're given to garden parties, it just might join in – Brazilians love a good party (think carnival). Its compact shape makes it a good candidate for the conservatory, if yours is bright – and very high!

BRAHEA ARMATA

Common name: Mexican blue palm
Place of origin: California
Hardiness rating: to -10°C when mature
Eventual height: about 3m (10m)

THIS IS A true blueblood amongst palms. Yup, its leaves really are pale blue. Which makes it particularly useful because if you're finding your exotic planting is all looking a bit, well, green – you know how all those bananas and gingers can end up rather samey – it's the perfect way to introduce some variation without resorting to variegation. What's more, not content with being a must-have because of its stunning blue leaves, *Brahea armata's* stiff fans are very finely cut to give the whole plant a really rather exquisitely aristocratic appearance. All you have to do now is find a sunny, well-drained spot in your garden, then give it lots of water in summer, and keep it drier in winter.

PHOENIX CANARIENSIS

Common name: Canary Island date palm
Place of origin: the name rather gives it away
Hardiness rating: to -18°C when mature
Eventual height: 16m (60ft)

AS PALMS go, this one's quite sprightly. It's also as Mediterranean as Monte Carlo. If you've been haunting garden centres this year, these palms seem to be everywhere you turn. But forget those tiddlers. You need a big specimen if you're thinking of planting it out. Last year I invested £70 in one that's about 1.5m (5ft) tall from top to toe, with maybe 15cm (6in) of trunk, and even that's not really big enough. People who know about these things have suggested I don't get too attached to it – one, woundingly, called it 'bedding' – but during the winter it just sailed through a -6°C frost unscathed and totally unprotected, and I'm hugging myself. It wants a spot in a mild garden, in full sun and rich loamy soil. Mine seems pretty blasé about coastal gales.

WASHINGTON FILIFERA

Common name: Cotton palm
Place of origin: West coast of USA and Mexico
Hardiness rating: to -8°C when mature
Eventual height: 16m (60ft)

WASHINGTONIA FILIFERA is either the 'big hair' palm – or the 'bad hair day' palm – I can't make my mind up, though it's definitely a blonde and therefore lots of fun. Those peculiar white hairs which decorate the shiny fan-shaped leaves certainly put it in a league of its own. Like all the most popular blondes, it's cheap and rather fast – more Diana Dors than Doris Day. It also enjoys a drink: don't be fooled by their desert origins, these palms are really thirsty. Trouble is, -8°C isn't really all that cold. If it helps, a year or so ago I came upon a web site that told of a man growing them successfully in Austria with the help of heated wires. Strange but true.

Where to pick up a palm

THERE ARE a few things you should know before abandoning yourself to the pleasures of the palm. First, they're slow. They're not for Christmas, they're for life, so buy the biggest you can afford. And because they're slow, they're not cheap, so save up.

The flip side of this is that at least they're pretty low maintenance. Just water and feed them copiously in summer, and maybe give them a bit of frost protection, and they'll sit there quite happily.

The next thing to consider is just how lucky do you feel? Some palms are hardier than others, so the more inclined you are to push the boundaries of hardiness, the more choice you've got.

All the palms shown here have pretty impressive frost-hardiness credentials, but bear in mind that, generally speaking, the bigger the plant, the hardier it'll be. I have a *Washingtonia filifera* sitting on my coffee table, waiting till it's put on a bit of size before I dare plant it out. There's also evidence to suggest that palms which are growing vigorously through the autumn are hardier.

When it comes to buying palms, you won't get very far at your average garden centre. The exception to this rule is *Trachycarpus fortunei* which is pretty widely available, sometimes as larger specimens. *Chamaerops humilis*, which is just as tough, is also not too tricky to come across nowadays. But if you feel like experimenting with other palms, you'll need a specialist nursery.

The good news is that nurseries concentrating on exotics and palms are proliferating. To get you going, here are four well worth considering. They all have catalogues and do mail order:

● **Architectural Plants**, Cooks Farm, Nuthurst, W Sussex RH13 6LH tel: 01403 891772. It's well worth visiting their web site at www.gardening-uk.com/architectural_plants
● **Mulu Nurseries**, Burford House, Tenbury Wells, Worcestershire WR15 8HQ tel: 01584 811592. Its web site is at www.mulu.co.uk
● **The Palm Centre**, Ham Nursery, Ham Street, Ham, Richmond, Surrey TW10 7HA tel: 0181 255 6191. Its web site is at www.palmcentre.co.uk
● **The Palm Farm**, Thornton Hall Gardens, Ulceby, N. Linc DN39 6XF tel/fax: 01469 531232

Palm court orc

Martin Gibbons matches 'parlour' palms to conservatory environments to put a modern twist on Victorian style

"Woe betide he or she who tries to maintain humidity by sloshing water about!"

LEFT: *Chamaedorea elegans*

The Victorians really had it made! Great glass palaces both public and private, roaring furnaces powered by cheap coal to keep them warm, servants a-plenty to keep them maintained and, above all, a huge selection of tropical plants from the expanding empire – from India, from Africa and from South America.

These days, alas, we have to be a little more modest. For who can afford fuel to maintain stove-house temperatures in winter? And who has servants to look after them? Most 'glass palaces' nowadays are 6 by 10ft greenhouses or conservatories, which are in reality extensions to the house complete with carpets and upholstered furniture. Woe betide he or she who tries to maintain humidity by sloshing water about!

What we have retained from Victorian times is the huge selection of plants available, and in this respect we are incredibly lucky; among them are plants for every condition, every corner and every climate, from humid stove house to arid conservatory, to glasshouses that are like a furnace by day and a fridge by night.

Among the most popular of conservatory plants are palms. While most people imagine palms to come from blazing deserts – some do, of course – most are not happy in the hot, dry and bright atmosphere of the normal conservatory.

The list of suitable candidates is, however, lengthened dramatically if some sort of shading is employed. It might be the spray-on kind which is applied to the outside of the glass, or the more attractive interior muslin-on-wires which takes the edge off the glare and reproduces the perfect light in which most palms will thrive: bright but direct.

Having reduced the summer light levels to something more friendly for our palms, we need to consider the temperature levels. These can soar during a sunny June day when the occupiers are at work and all the windows are closed.

Not all plants will enjoy these extreme

hestra

conditions, so consider having a small, thermostatically controlled extractor fan fitted high up in the ridge.

When the temperature reaches a certain level, the fan will click in, extracting all the rising hot air, and sucking in cooler air, perhaps from a ground-level vent, to replace it.

Many palms will tolerate high temperatures and even bright light as long as the humidity doesn't drop too low, but the heat of the summer can literally squeeze every drop of moisture from the atmosphere, and dry out our precious palms like washing on a line.

Humidifiers

The best, but inevitably most expensive alternative, is an electric humidifier, the modern equivalent of the old habit of

LEFT:
*Chamaerops
humilis*

LEFT: *Kentia
(syn. howea) fosteriana*

In a perfect palm world

If your conservatory has a stone floor and no furniture to worry about, where, with regular damping down – OK, sloshing lots of water around – you can maintain a humid atmosphere, and if you can afford to keep up the temperatures in winter and can shade out the harsh sunlight, then the world is your oyster when it comes to growing palms indoors.

Choose from the steamy jungles of Asia or the cloud forest of the Andes, because there are literally hundreds of wonderful species which will thrive in such an environment.

Consider licuala, with its huge round and flat leaves measuring 120cm (4ft) across, areca and cyrtostachys, with brilliant red or orange crownshafts, tiny chamaedorea from Mexico, full grown at 60cm (2ft) tall, or the almost unpronounceable *Johannesteijsmannia altifrons* (Joey for short), with pleated, paddle-shaped leaves that as are hard as cardboard.

'damping down' – tricky when there are carpets and furniture to consider. Expensive to buy but cheap to run, they will prove to be of enormous benefit not only to the plants but to people too, and provide a much more comfortable atmosphere for all living things.

Failing that, water-filled dishes of pebbles placed all around are better than nothing – the speed with which the water will be seen to evaporate will give an indication of the dryness of the air.

Having discussed the environment and conditions that most palms will prefer, let's take a look at the plants themselves and try to prove my 'every condition, every climate' claim.

The natural habitat of the palm gives the best clue as to its suitability for one environment over another. Despite what has been said, desert palms for example will indeed thrive in the hot, dry and bright conservatory that's furnace-like by day and like a fridge at night since that's what their desert home is like.

They have the added benefit of being extremely cold hardy, so can usually be planted in the garden when and if they get too big for use indoors.

Most of us are unable to provide an all-round perfect environment, but I hope you will be able to see from those listed below that there are palms for everyone and every location. Though we may not have the resources our of Victorian forebears, they would surely approve of our modern use of indoor palms.

Brahea armata

One of the best palms is *Brahea armata*, the Mexican blue fan palm from the south-west United States and northern Mexico.

More and more commonly seen in garden centres and specialist nurseries, it has attractive, ice-blue, fan-shaped leaves, perhaps 60cm (2ft) across. It's not a fast grower, so is ideal for the conservatory where it will take a number of years to outgrow its welcome. In the south, at least, it makes a stunning addition to the sunny garden, where it will ultimately grow to a good size.

Blue Med fan palm

Somewhat more modest in size is the 'new' palm that's on everyone's lips. It goes by the name of *Chamaerops humilis var. cerifera*, though perhaps blue Mediterranean fan palm is easier to remember.

Related to the well-known green form of chamaerops, it probably deserves species status. It was almost unknown in cultivation until a few years ago when expedition members found it growing in enormous numbers in the High Atlas Mountains of Morocco. Quite why it is not more common in cultivation is a total mystery. Fortunately, it is now increasingly being seen in garden centres and is set to become extremely popular once it is more widely available.

A third of the size of the Mexican palm, above, it has small fan-shaped leaves of the same ice-blue colour. Again, it's not a fast grower, but perhaps that is a benefit in view of the size of most glasshouses. Its steady growth will be appreciated as each blue leaf opens, and it too is extremely hardy, so is ideal for planting out in the garden when it has attained some size.

Phoenix canariensis

Like the two palms above, *Phoenix canariensis* (Canary Island date palm) will thrive in the hot, dry, bright conservatory

LEFT: *Phoenix canariensis*

> **"The heat of the summer can literally squeeze every drop of moisture from the atmosphere, and dry out our precious palms like washing on a line"**

even where there is no shading, no ventilation and irregular watering.

It will also put up with extreme cold in the winter. Unlike them, it is a feather palm – having a central stem, with leaflets coming off it like a feather – and can grow rather fast, attaining a good size in just a few years.

It has attractive, bright green foliage and, in nature at least, forms a stout trunk. Its Mediterranean appearance is accentuated when it is planted in a terracotta pot, and it looks wonderful, too, stood out on the terrace in summer.

The somewhat spiny leaflets towards the base of each leaf may put some prospective owners off. This, however, would be a great shame as its easy nature, durability and tolerance of extreme conditions, complimented by its handsome appearance, make it one of the most suitable palms for indoor use.

Kentia palm

For many people the kentia palm is 'the' palm tree for indoor enjoyment. Famous since the Victorians used it for their palm court orchestras, it comes from just one tiny spot in the middle of the ocean, Lord Howe Island, off the north-east coast of Australia.

It does not enjoy bright light, but is tolerant of other less than ideal conditions; just imagine the gas heating and lighting, and all that cigar smoke they would have had to put up with in their Victorian heyday! With some shading, an abundance of water, and a regular but light feed, the kentia will thrive outdoors.

It is hard to imagine a more elegant and genteel palm that is absolutely synonymous with the conservatory, whatever its proportions.

Phoenix rebellenii

Another favourite indoor palm is a diminutive and tropical relative of the Canary Island date, *Phoenix rebellenii* (pigmy date palm).

We are moving now into the territory of palms that are slightly more fussy about the conditions in which they are grown. While still easy to care for, the pigmy date palm enjoys an abundance of moisture at its roots and indeed, in hot weather, can safely be stood in a dish of water which is topped up every day.

From Laos in south-east Asia, it grows in nature on the banks of the Mekong River and is inundated every year during the wet season.

Pretty and jaunty, it is in many ways a miniature version of the perfect palm. Usually purchased as a stemless rosette of fine feather leaves, in time it grows a slim trunk and reaches a maximum height of but a few feet.

VERTICAL EXOTICS

Bractically speaking

Have you noticed that every hot holiday destination's airport has a bougainvillea waiting to greet you? **Mike Pilcher** suggests brightening up our conservatories with some colourful papery bracts

For me, the twining bougainvillea, or paper flower, immediately conjures up thoughts of mild climates and tropical shores.

I've had something of a love/hate relationship with these scrubby scramblers since I first encountered them growing as wild as I was in the south of Spain. Native to tropical and sub-tropical South America, they seemed just as at home on the Costa del Something, smothering walls and fences in colours that would rival even the showiest azaleas and rhododendrons.

They're named after Louis Antoin, Compte de Bougainville (1729-1811) who brought them to Europe from Brazil around 1767. Their bracts – modified leaves carried just behind the inconspicuous tubular flowers – range from pure white, through cream and pink, pale orange and yellow to deep red, crimson, purple and magenta. They're the sort of colours you only usually see together on *Changing Rooms*, but in this instance they work rather well.

In favoured locations, not bothered by frosts let alone snow, bougainvilleas remain evergreen throughout the year, producing sporadic splashes of colour that seduce the holidaymaker and gardener alike.

Back home, they're sadly too tender to survive if planted outside, but they do make superb specimens for the cool greenhouse or conservatory. Here, the fragility of their showy bracts and their willingness to scramble up and over anything within reach provides colour from early spring right through to late autumn. And if you can keep the temperature above 4°C

Cultivation and care in the cool conservatory

- Minimum daytime temperatures 5-10°C
- Minimum night-time temperature 2°C
- Ideal summer temperatures 18°C and above
- Repot in spring if necessary using a John Innes No1 potting compost
- Pot-bound plants will flower and produce bracts more readily
- Mist leaves and bracts to maintain humidity and help prevent red spider mite
- Some tying up will be necessary. A trellis frame will help
- Water well from spring through to autumn when the plants are growing vigorously
- Use a balanced fertiliser in early spring, and in summer switch to a high-potash fertiliser such as a tomato food. Bougainvilleas are greedy plants so it's difficult to over feed them
- Water sparingly during the winter when plants are not actively growing

ABOVE: The salmon bronze 'Louis Watten'

'Miss Manila' – one of the oldest and loveliest bougainvilleas – will lend its beauty to your conservatory

PICTURES: HARRY SMITH COLLECTION

ABOVE: Yellow is a less common colour – this is 'Golden Glow'

Shock tactics

Bougainvilleas can be a little difficult to achieve repeat flowering. If yours has plenty of leaves but no flowers or bracts, try shocking it into action:
■ **Allow the plant to dry out and wilt slightly before rewatering**
■ **Use a high-potash fertiliser**
■ **Make sure the plant gets plenty of sunlight**
■ **Train new growth horizontally. This encourages more lateral growth and therefore more flowers and bracts – rather like training a climbing rose**

the plants will remain evergreen.

I said love/hate relationship because in the past I've tried to grow several bougainvilleas in pots at home, and had some spectacular failures. They started off full of exotic promise fresh from the garden centre, but within weeks they looked pale, tired and started to drop their bracts and leaves.

Pruning tips

ANY VIGOROUS climber growing in the cool conservatory will need some judicious pruning. Bougainvilleas are no exception, and it's best to wear gloves when handling the thorny stems. Make sure secateurs are clean and sharp. Plants flower (and bract) well whether they are pruned or not, but it's worth noting that the flowers and bracts are produced on the previous season's growth so it's best to prune after flowering. February is ideal.
1. Start by cutting weak or straggly shoots back to the main stem, leaving two or three buds to encourage new lateral growth
2. Main leaders can be left unpruned until the required framework is achieved
3. Trim back sideshoots to two buds to encourage new growth and subsequent flowering
4. If space is very limited, keep the plant in a more shrubby form by regular pruning and pinching out of the shoot tips

Full sun lovers

My problem, it seemed, was that I was trying to grow them as house plants rather than conservatory plants, and I quickly realised that my windows were too small for my house.

These plants like full sun – and plenty of it. The cool conservatory or greenhouse offer ideal conditions.

The word 'climber' is a little over-generous. Bougainvilleas tend to sprawl, throwing their shoots over adjacent plants for additional support. In among the leaves are small – but ever so efficient – thorns that help attach them to their neighbours – and you. You have been warned.

Plants can easily reach a height of 6m (20ft), hence the need for some disciplinary pruning in the average conservatory. Left to air their bracts untended they'll soon take over, but can provide valuable shade for sun-shy plants – and humans. However, remember to give plenty of ventilation otherwise the papery bracts will get cooked in high temperatures.

Although garden centres tend to stock unnamed varieties, they're usually cheap and well worth buying. From specialist suppliers you'll find a much wider range of hybrids in varying colours. Most have the toughest crimson species *B. glabra* as a parent. Names to look out for include the

ABOVE: 'Raspberry Ice' is a variegated form

ABOVE: A typical street scene in Spain, where bougainvillea can be trimmed into a fairly formal hedge

ABOVE: There are many coloured forms of the Brazilian *Bougainvillea spectabilis*

salmon bronze 'Louis Watten', pink-and-white 'Turkish Delight', yellow 'Golden Glow', rose-pink 'Miss Manila', and the pink 'Brilliance Variegata' which has green-and-white variegated leaves adding to the cast list.

So, we have one of the showiest climbers you'll find that requires frost-free growing conditions, plenty of summer sun – and quite a bit of room. Even better is the fact that they're perfect for growing in containers so you can move them outside onto the patio or terrace during the summer, or plunge them in beds and borders among other hardier exotics. It's also a great way of keeping their vigorous growth in check.

Go on, treat yourself to one of the brightest, bractiest plants you'll ever come across. You'll not regret it.

Pests and disease

BOUGAINVILLEAS are robust plants and therefore little worried by any major pests and diseases. Remember, a healthily growing plant is less likely to encounter problems.
Look out for signs of whitefly, mealy bug, red spider mite and aphids, particularly on new shoot tips. Whitefly and red spider mite will be more evident in hot, dry conditions while mealy-bugs and aphids prefer it warm and humid. Control can easily be achieved with a preparatory pesticide or by adopting a more environmental approach with biological controls. Misting regularly will help, as will good ventilation on hot, summer days.

"They're the sort of colours you only usually see together on *Changing Rooms* but in this instance they work rather well"

Buying bougainvilleas by mail order

Conservatory Plant Line, West Bergholt, Colchester, Essex CO6 3DH, tel 01206 242 533

Fleur de Lys, Restharrow Cottage, Lower Street, Fittleworth, West Sussex RH20 1EL, tel 01798 865 475

The Conservatory, Station Road, Gomshall, Nr Dorking, Surrey GU5 9LB, tel 01483 203 019

Westdale Nurseries, Holt Road, Bradford-upon-Avon, Wilts BA15 1TS, tel 01225 863 258

Propagation

BOUGAINVILLEAS can be propagated from cuttings, although it can be a little tricky. In spring you can take softwood cuttings, in the summer semi-ripe and in the autumn hardwood cuttings. For all three types, start by selecting a healthy shoot approx. 5-8cm (2-3in) long. Cut the base cleanly with a sharp knife just below a node (leaf joint) and the top just above a bud. Remove the lower leaves and dip the bottom end in hormone-rooting powder. Inset around the sides of a pot of gritty seed and cutting compost. Firm and water.
■ Softwood cuttings should be covered with a plastic bag and given a little bottom heat to encourage rooting. Open the bag occasionally to let out excess moisture which could cause rotting.
■ Semi-ripe cuttings can be taken with a heel (small sliver of the parent stem) and left to root in a cold frame during the summer.
Hardwood cuttings should be placed in a frost-free conservatory or on a windowsill for the winter and should have rooted by early spring.

Chlorophytum
hangs magnificently
below a colourful
balcony of flowers

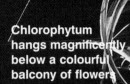

Hanging baskets
containing tropical plants
can give a new dimension
to porch or conservatory.
Roger Sweetinburgh
has some exciting
suggestions

Basket
cases

HARRY SMITH COLLECTION

While bright red pelargoniums give an authentic flavour of the Mediterranean, and will happily go outside in hanging baskets in the summer, arguably they are not very exotic. Lovely yes, prolifically flowering yes, but daringly different, well, to be brutally honest… no.

So how about planting up some baskets with jungly tropicals that will lift the sightlines in your greenhouse or conservatory.

There is just one proviso, however: all the plants growing together in one basket must be tolerant of the same growing conditions.

All my choices will need regular feeding during the summer with a balanced plant food containing trace elements.

Although wire baskets lined with sphagnum moss are used here, plastic hanging containers could also be used.

Use a 50/50 mixture of soilless compost and John Innes potting compost and make sure it is fairly well compacted after planting as loose compost dries out too quickly.

Leave room for watering in

"How about planting up some baskets with jungly tropicals that will lift the sightlines in your green-house or conservatory"

LEFT: Exotic *Russellia equisetiformis*

Basket 1

This basket is planted with just two different plants, *Setcretesia pallida* 'Purple Heart' and *Syngonium podophyllum*. Both prefer to be indoors and the syngonium needs quite humid conditions.

They both like bright light – not direct sunlight – and to be kept fairly moist during the growing season – drier during the winter.

Setcresia is not generally grown as a trailing plant although it does spread and is ideal for the centre of a basket where it can sprawl sideways as well as provide some height.

The purple 'tradescantia'-shaped leaves contrast well with the small pink flowers as well as with the foliage of the syngonium, but eventually the longest shoots will become too leggy and have to be cut back.

Syngonium's natural tendency is to climb, but in the absence of a pole it will happily trail over the edge of a pot or basket. Smaller, less spear-shaped leaves are produced on trailing growth than on climbing growth but all have an attractive variegation which makes them look as if they have been sprayed with a light, almost flu-

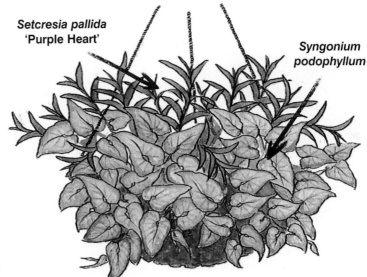

Setcresia pallida 'Purple Heart'

Syngonium podophyllum

orescent emerald-green paint.

Unfortunately, the leaves could be damaged by rough weather conditions if grown outside and they are sometimes vulnerable to aphids.

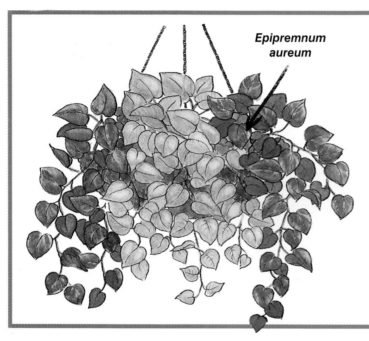

Epipremnum aureum

Basket 2

There is just one type of plant here, *Epipremnum aureum*. This must be one of the easiest 'indoor' plants to grow. Although it will readily climb a pole, it is equally happy trailing from baskets and troughs.

The basic leaf colour is a dark glossy green but many leaves are streaked yellow and there is a golden form – often lime green in poor light.

I have seen this plant trailing from troughs high up in a hot sunny atrium and, as happily, growing in a relatively dark room at least 3m (10ft) from the nearest window. In good light – though preferably not scorching sunlight – the trailing branches can exceed 1.5m (5ft).

While it is growing vigorously during the summer, epipremnum needs constant moisture and regular feeding, but in winter the plant can be kept relatively dry with no feeding. It can be grown outdoors during the summer, but only in a very sheltered spot and preferably in a porch or on a veranda.

PICTURES: ROGER SWEETINBURGH

Basket 3

Here is another basket which relies solely on foliage colour for its effect. It uses two different plants, *Gynura aurantiaca* and *Tradescantia fluminensis* 'Variegata'.

Gynura is unusual in that it has leaves which are deep purple and hairy. The hairs are more pink than purple, giving the new leaves an almost luminous glow.

It is not a trailing plant but, like setcresia, it is ideal for the centre of a basket where it can spread in all directions. Some shoots will grow to a height of about 20cms (8ins) before producing some yellowy-orange flowers. These smell very

unpleasant and are best removed before they open!

Although gynura is tolerant of poor light, it develops a stronger colour in bright light. It should be kept damp during the summer and relatively dry in winter and although it will tolerate a warm sheltered spot outdoors for the summer, it is best kept indoors all the year round.

All tradescantias are easy to grow. This one will happily share the same conditions as the gynura and produce a mass of trailing growth throughout the summer. The leaves are striped green, white and pink and are therefore a perfect foil for the deep

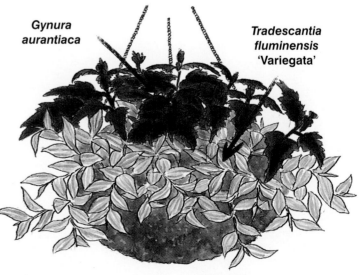

Gynura aurantiaca

Tradescantia fluminensis 'Variegata'

purple gynura.

It is important to feed tradescantias when they are growing fast to prevent the older leaves from dying off. Good light will ensure that growth is not too leggy and that the leaf colour is maintained.

"I have seen this plant trailing from troughs high up in a hot sunny atrium and growing in a relatively dark room at least 3m from the nearest window"

LEFT: 'Hot' hanging basket of *Lotus berthelotii*

the top of the basket or place a small plastic funnel discretely among the plants so that you can pour water into this.

Wire baskets lined with moss provide you with the opportunity to have some plants growing out from the sides of the basket.

Some of the schemes featured here will be best viewed at eye level rather than from below, so vary the height at which you hang your baskets according to what you have planted in them.

Take great care handling prickly or hairy plants especially if you have sensitive skin.

Rain water is generally better for containerised plants than tap water which can be highly alkaline.

Systemic insecticides can be very effective in controlling pests on indoor plants. They are sometimes available in the form of 'plant pins' which are pushed into the compost to release small amounts of systemic insecticide every time the plant is watered. But always read the label before using these products.

Basket 4

This basket contains three different plants, *Chlorophytum comosum* 'Vittatum', *Campanula isophylla* and *Begonia sutherlandii*.

All three could quite easily be grown outdoors in a porch for the summer but would have to be brought indoors for the winter.

Chlorophytum is one of the best-known houseplants and is valuable here for its brightly variegated foliage. Although not strictly a trailing plant, it does produce plantlets on the end of long arching stems. It will tolerate both wet and dry soil as well as a wide range of temperature.

Campanula isophylla is an easy plant to grow, again being tolerant of a wide range of conditions. It flowers for several weeks during the summer but does need good light to do so. Although it will grow outdoors in summer it prefers fairly high humidity and will not apreciate being lashed by wind and rain. It can be kept indoors through the winter but it is often best to start each year with new plants.

The remarkably adaptable *Begonia sutherlandii* is unusual in having orange flowers which, in this scheme, contrast well

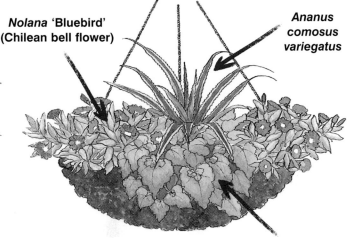

Chlorophytum comosum 'Vittatum'

Campanula isophylla

Begonia sutherlandii

with the blue campanula. Its weeping habit makes it ideal for a basket where it should continue to flower well into the autumn before dying back to a corm for the winter.

It dislikes being wet so if grown outdoors for the summer it should be kept out of the rain. During the winter the dormant corms need to be kept cool and dry.

Nephrolepsis exaltata (sword fern)

Basket 5

There is just one plant in this basket – *Nephrolepis exaltata* (sword fern). This, along with many other ferns, needs constant humidity and moisture as well as somewhere sheltered, away from direct sunlight. This basket should therefore be kept in a warm, humid greenhouse or conservatory, summer and winter.

As the plant develops, its leaves will hang down and partly cover the sides of the basket. Dry, draughty conditions can cause the tips of older leaves to turn brown, but apart from this it is one of the easiest ferns to grow.

"Take great care handling prickly or hairy plants especially if you have sensitive skin"

Nolana 'Bluebird' (Chilean bell flower)

Ananus comosus variegatus

Tolmiea menziesii 'Gold Splash' (pick-a-back- plant)

Basket 6

There are three different plants here, *Ananus comosus* 'Variegatus', *Nolana* 'Bluebird', and *Tolmiea menzeisii* 'Gold Splash'.

Ananus is the pineapple and this form, with its attractively variegated leaves, is ideal as the centrepiece of a basket. It does prefer good light, fairly high temperatures and high humidity so it should not be grown outdoors in the summer.

It is also essential that other plants growing alongside will enjoy or tolerate the same conditions. In winter it can be kept drier and less humid but still warm.

Nolana is a hardy annual that is often grown outdoors for the summer but also under glass. Although it does not need high humidity, it will grow happily in this basket alongside the ananus so long as it is not constantly misted.

It is a trailing plant so will soon cascade down over the sides and flower for most of the summer. It is better to grow new plants from seed each spring than to try and overwinter them.

Tolmiea will also grow outdoors in the summer but is ideal for this basket since it will also thrive in warm bright conditions under glass. The plants will soon grow over the edge and part way down the sides of the basket, contrasting well with the flowers and foliage of the nolana. Tiny plantlets are produced on top of the older leaves, making it very easy to propagate.

Passiflora mollissima is every bit as gorgeous as P. x alato-cerulia

Social climbers

Climbers aren't just for walls. They can make even the dullest shrub or tree look jubilantly jungly. Peter Reid goes upwardly mobile

There's one in every garden. I have several in mine. I'm talking about those big shrubs or small trees which, around this time of year, look like a waste of space.

It's not their fault. They do their bit to hide the fences and give the garden a bit of privacy. They even flower... and that's the main problem.

Because, you see, they flower in spring. Which means

that now, just as the rest of the garden is busting out in a carnival of tropical colour, there they sit, big blobs of green. I'm sorry, but they really don't bring much to the party.

You could dig them out and start again, I suppose, but I don't have the heart. Nor the energy. Besides, there's an easier way. Simply pop a summer-flowering climber up them.

You'll get double the flowers for the same space – some-

thing dear to most gardeners' hearts – plus extra flower power during your tropical garden's peak period.

And all those twining stems and contrasting foliage will add to the congestion that's all part of the jungly mood – trellis and south-facing walls are a bit thin on the ground in rainforests.

To get you going, here's a handful of suggestions for social climbers which like to

hang out with other plants. When choosing a climber, there's only one rule to remember: if the tree or shrub is evergreen, choose an evergreen climber or you'll get a brown mess when the climber loses its leaves. For deciduous trees or shrubs, you can use evergreen or deciduous climbers.

There again, in exotic gardening, rules are made to be broken. Onwards and upwards...

PASSIONS RUN HIGH

PASSIFLORA MOLLISSIMA
Common name: banana passion flower
Place of origin: the Americas
Hardiness rating: to -5° C

THIS ISSUE'S front cover shows *Passiflora x alato-cerulia* – gorgeous, isn't it? But my particular passion is *Passiflora mollissima*. Its pink flowers are large and showy, it has nice three-lobed evergreen leaves and, being tall, it can make an impression on even big shrubs. Best of all, though, is the yellow fruit which, as well as being large and edible, is shaped like a banana... and you can't get more exotic than that. All passion flowers are on the tender side – mollissima is as hardy as most – but if you live in a cold area it makes an ideal conservatory plant. They're easy to look after – plant them in the borders, or in any standard potting mixture in tubs or large pots. To prune, thin out the main stems and cut back the remaining laterals.

ABOVE: *Passiflora mollissima*

BRASSY TRUMPETS

ABOVE: Campsis grandiflora

CAMPSIS GRANDIFLORA
Common name: chinese trumpet creeper
Place of origin: China
Hardiness rating: fairly hardy

CAMPSIS RADICANS is more common and a bit hardier, but if you want bigger flowers, then go for *Campsis grandiflora*. It produces flowers that are 5-9cm (2-3¾in) long in big terminal trusses. They're a deep, hot orange, with a red-veined throat that are as exotic as all-get-out in late summer to autumn. The deciduous leaves, made up of about seven leaflets, are also pretty fetching. This is a big plant – up to 10m (33ft) or more – so it needs a decent-sized tree to get to grips with... your neighbour's ley-landii springs to mind – forget what I said about planting evergreen with evergreen. It wants heat to ripen, so if you're in a cool area it'll need full sun. It also benefits from shelter and some tying because it's not over-blessed with aerial roots. Otherwise, just give it moisture-retentive but well-drained humus-rich soil and prune in spring if it gets too big by cutting all last year's growth back to two pairs of buds.

ALSTROEMERIAS IN THE SKY

BOMAREA MULTIFLORA
Common name: climbing alstroemeria
Place of origin: South America
Hardiness rating: at least -4° C

BOMAREA REALLY is rather a special climber, perfect for a medium-sized shrub with preferably dark foliage to set off the umbels of flowers. These vary from bright red to salmon-orange, almost always with yellow centres spotted with chocolate which are easily visible because you look up into them. Planted outside in a sheltered spot, it flowers from mid-summer to winter – I've seen its flowers with snow on them in December. It gets to a maximum of about three metres outside.

If the temperature drops below -4° C it becomes deciduous, but stays ever-green in a conservatory. It becomes dormant in winter – don't we all? – then sends up six or so shoots in spring which need to be protected from slug attack.

After flowering, cut out the dead stems. If you think multiflora too tender for your area, try isopetala which seems able to take more frost without damage.

RIGHT: *Bomarea caldasii*

FLORIDA FLAVOUR

CLEMATIS FLORIDA SIEBOLDII

Common name: none
Place of origin: China
Hardiness rating: hardy

THERE ARE about 200 climbing clematis to choose from, so take your pick. Something blousy like Vivyan Pennell could tempt me, or the useful evergreen winter-flowering cirrhosa, but for sheer glamour take a look at *Clematis florida sieboldii*. Can you resist its white-with-a-hint-of-green flowers with those rosettes of purple stamens? It flowers late spring to early summer and might give you a few blooms later. Even better, it's not too vigorous – up to 4m (13ft) – and doesn't really need much in the way of pruning, although any tidying up should be done in late winter before it starts growing. The foliage is deciduous or partly evergreen. Plant it in full sun or partial shade, with its roots and base in shade and moist but well drained soil.

RIGHT: *Clematis florida sieboldii*

LEFT: *Lonicera japonica aureoreticulata*

IT'S A HONEY

LONICERA JAPONICA AUREORETICULATA

Common name: Variegated honeysuckle
Place of origin: Japan, Korea, China
Hardiness rating: hardy

I know what you're thinking – what's exotic about a honeysuckle? Well, its vigorous twining stems which can take it to a height of 10m (33ft) or more give it a tropical mood. But what really sets this honeysuckle apart is that it's evergreen and its leaves are decorated with a network of golden veins, making it a useful foliage contrast plant. It would look good against dark green foliage, but I have one climbing through the dark purple-brown leaves of a *Cotinus coggygria* 'Grace' where, as well as the striking colour contrast, it gives the deciduous cotinus some much needed and rather fetching tie-dye-style winter clothing through the winter. Add to that, creamy white summer flowers which age to yellow, and fragrance to boot, and it earns its place in my tropical border.

PURPLE PASSAGE

LESPEDEZA THUNBERGII

Common name: bush clover
Place of origin: North China and Japan
Hardiness rating: hardy

THIS ISN'T actually a climber, but if you want to brighten up a smallish spring-flowering shrub like an azalea or, in my case, a *Daphne odora*, it's particularly good value. Plant it beneath your shrub and then wait for it to erupt in summer, shooting its gangly, arching branches up to 3m (9½ft) long through the shrub which it leans on for support. The leaves aren't up to much but, in late summer it bears big clustered racemes of rose-purple pea-like flowers and looks for all the world like a very untidy purple fountain. Its stems are herbaceous and die back to a woody rootstock in winter. It's not a difficult plant, but it does like a humus-rich well-drained soil in sun.

ABOVE: *Lespedeza thunbergii*

Climbing tip

If you're thinking of planting Golden Hop (*Humulus lupulus* 'Aureus'), think twice, or put it in a pot. With its bronze-red stems and gold leaves, it's a seductive plant, but it's a devil to dig out. Tugging out its thick, bendy fibrous roots is like pulling on a hemp rope, and they tend to shred, leaving you with more plants than you started with.

"*Campsis grandiflora* is a big plant so it needs a decent-sized tree to get to grips with... your neighbour's leylandii springs to mind"

UNDIGNIFIED SCRAMBLE

TROPAEOLUM SPECIOSUM

Common name: flame creeper or flame nasturtium
Place of origin: Chile
Hardiness rating: hardy

THIS HERBACEOUS perennial is a riot of red from mid summer to mid autumn when it's covered in vermilion-scarlet flowers, followed by blue seeds. Before that, its little light green six-lobed leaves aren't bad either, especially if you put it into a shrub with dark evergreen foliage. It tolerates full sun, but can be a bit of a prima donna about where you plant it because it likes a cool root run in moist, but not wet, acid soil and partial shade. Its new growth is also vulnerable to slugs. The slender stems grow from a creeping rhizome and can get to a height of about 3-4.5m (9-15ft). Delight and impress your friends by pointing out that its name comes from the Latin 'tropaeum', meaning 'trophy', because it reminded Linnaeus of a battlefield trophy pillar hung with the shields (the round leaves) and bloody helmets (the red flowers) of the vanquished. Mm, Linnaeus must've had a lively imagination.

RIGHT: *Tropaeolum speciosum*

"Mm, Linnaeus must've had a lively imagination"

GOURD, THE BAD AND THE UGLY

CUCURBITA PEPO

Common name: ornamental gourds
Country of origin: the Americas
Hardiness rating: none

Love them or loathe them, you can't deny that few things could look more startlingly tropical than a crop of ornamental gourds hanging off something like a rhododendron, arbutus or magnolia. And, of course, these are true exotics, coming mainly from the tropical and subtropical areas of the American continent. Sow them as annuals – outdoors in May to June – in a prepared seed bed where you want them to do their stuff, then train the new seedlings up your shrub or tree. You should have floppy yellow flowers in summer, followed in late summer to autumn by the fruits which come in all sorts of dramatic colorations. If you want warts and all, Johnsons Seeds do packs of Small Warted Hybrids.

ABOVE: *Cucurbita pepo*

Did you know?

The passion flower's name has nothing to do with infatuation, though it's all too easy to get a crush on them. Deriving from the Latin 'passio', meaning 'passion', and 'flos', meaning 'flower', it was given its name by missionaries who saw the arrangement of its floral organs as symbolic of Christ's crucifixion: the three knobbed styles stand for the three nails; the five anthers recall the five wounds; and the corona symbolises the crown of thorns.

INDEX

(Page numbers in bold refer to illustrations.)

TITLES AVAILABLE FROM
GMC Publications
BOOKS

WOODCARVING

Beginning Woodcarving	GMC Publications
Carving Architectural Detail in Wood: The Classical Tradition	Frederick Wilbur
Carving Birds & Beasts	GMC Publications
Carving the Human Figure: Studies in Wood and Stone	Dick Onians
Carving Nature: Wildlife Studies in Wood	Frank Fox-Wilson
Carving on Turning	Chris Pye
Decorative Woodcarving	Jeremy Williams
Elements of Woodcarving	Chris Pye
Essential Woodcarving Techniques	Dick Onians
Lettercarving in Wood: A Practical Course	Chris Pye
Making & Using Working Drawings for Realistic Model Animals	
	Basil F. Fordham
Power Tools for Woodcarving	David Tippey
Relief Carving in Wood: A Practical Introduction	Chris Pye
Understanding Woodcarving in the Round	GMC Publications
Useful Techniques for Woodcarvers	GMC Publications
Woodcarving: A Foundation Course	Zoë Gertner
Woodcarving for Beginners	GMC Publications
Woodcarving Tools, Materials & Equipment (New Edition in 2 vols.)	
	Chris Pye

WOODTURNING

Adventures in Woodturning	David Springett
Bowl Turning Techniques Masterclass	Tony Boase
Chris Child's Projects for Woodturners	Chris Child
Colouring Techniques for Woodturners	Jan Sanders
Contemporary Turned Wood: New Perspectives in a Rich Tradition	
	Ray Leier, Jan Peters & Kevin Wallace
The Craftsman Woodturner	Peter Child
Decorating Turned Wood: The Maker's Eye	Liz & Michael O'Donnell
Decorative Techniques for Woodturners	Hilary Bowen
Illustrated Woodturning Techniques	John Hunnex
Intermediate Woodturning Projects	GMC Publications
Keith Rowley's Woodturning Projects	Keith Rowley
Making Screw Threads in Wood	Fred Holder
Turned Boxes: 50 Designs	Chris Stott
Turning Green Wood	Michael O'Donnell
Turning Pens and Pencils	Kip Christensen & Rex Burningham
Useful Woodturning Projects	GMC Publications
Woodturning: Bowls, Platters, Hollow Forms, Vases, Vessels, Bottles, Flasks, Tankards, Plates	GMC Publications
Woodturning: A Foundation Course (New Edition)	Keith Rowley
Woodturning: A Fresh Approach	Robert Chapman
Woodturning: An Individual Approach	Dave Regester
Woodturning: A Source Book of Shapes	John Hunnex
Woodturning Jewellery	Hilary Bowen
Woodturning Masterclass	Tony Boase
Woodturning Techniques	GMC Publications

WOODWORKING

Advanced Scrollsaw Projects	GMC Publications
Beginning Picture Marquetry	Lawrence Threadgold
Bird Boxes and Feeders for the Garden	Dave Mackenzie
Celtic Carved Lovespoons: 30 Patterns	Sharon Littley & Clive Griffin
Celtic Woodcraft	Glenda Bennett
Complete Woodfinishing	Ian Hosker
David Charlesworth's Furniture-Making Techniques	David Charlesworth
David Charlesworth's Furniture-Making Techniques – Volume 2	
	David Charlesworth
The Encyclopedia of Joint Making	Terrie Noll
Furniture-Making Projects for the Wood Craftsman	GMC Publications
Furniture-Making Techniques for the Wood Craftsman	GMC Publications
Furniture Restoration (Practical Crafts)	Kevin Jan Bonner

Furniture Restoration: A Professional at Work	John Lloyd
Furniture Restoration and Repair for Beginners	Kevin Jan Bonner
Furniture Restoration Workshop	Kevin Jan Bonner
Green Woodwork	Mike Abbott
Intarsia: 30 Patterns for the Scrollsaw	John Everett
Kevin Ley's Furniture Projects	Kevin Ley
Making Chairs and Tables	GMC Publications
Making Chairs and Tables – Volume 2	GMC Publications
Making Classic English Furniture	Paul Richardson
Making Heirloom Boxes	Peter Lloyd
Making Little Boxes from Wood	John Bennett
Making Screw Threads in Wood	Fred Holder
Making Shaker Furniture	Barry Jackson
Making Woodwork Aids and Devices	Robert Wearing
Mastering the Router	Ron Fox
Pine Furniture Projects for the Home	Dave Mackenzie
Practical Scrollsaw Patterns	John Everett
Router Magic: Jigs, Fixtures and Tricks to Unleash your Router's Full Potential	Bill Hylton
Router Tips & Techniques	Robert Wearing
Routing: A Workshop Handbook	Anthony Bailey
Routing for Beginners	Anthony Bailey
Sharpening: The Complete Guide	Jim Kingshott
Sharpening Pocket Reference Book	Jim Kingshott
Simple Scrollsaw Projects	GMC Publications
Space-Saving Furniture Projects	Dave Mackenzie
Stickmaking: A Complete Course	Andrew Jones & Clive George
Stickmaking Handbook	Andrew Jones & Clive George
Storage Projects for the Router	GMC Publications
Test Reports: The Router and Furniture & Cabinetmaking	GMC Publications
Veneering: A Complete Course	Ian Hosker
Veneering Handbook	Ian Hosker
Woodfinishing Handbook (Practical Crafts)	Ian Hosker
Woodworking with the Router: Professional Router Techniques any Woodworker can Use	Bill Hylton & Fred Matlack

UPHOLSTERY

The Upholsterer's Pocket Reference Book	David James
Upholstery: A Complete Course (Revised Edition)	David James
Upholstery Restoration	David James
Upholstery Techniques & Projects	David James
Upholstery Tips and Hints	David James

TOYMAKING

Scrollsaw Toy Projects	Ivor Carlyle
Scrollsaw Toys for All Ages	Ivor Carlyle

CRAFTS

American Patchwork Designs in Needlepoint	Melanie Tacon
Beginning Picture Marquetry	Lawrence Threadgold
Blackwork: A New Approach	Brenda Day
Celtic Cross Stitch Designs	Carol Phillipson
Celtic Knotwork Designs	Sheila Sturrock
Celtic Knotwork Handbook	Sheila Sturrock
Celtic Spirals and Other Designs	Sheila Sturrock
Complete Pyrography	Stephen Poole
Creative Backstitch	Helen Hall
Creative Embroidery Techniques Using Colour Through Gold	
	Daphne J. Ashby & Jackie Woolsey
The Creative Quilter: Techniques and Projects	Pauline Brown
Cross-Stitch Designs from China	Carol Phillipson

GARDENING

PHOTOGRAPHY

ART TECHNIQUES

VIDEOS

MAGAZINES

WOODTURNING ◆ WOODCARVING
FURNITURE & CABINETMAKING
THE ROUTER ◆ NEW WOODWORKING
THE DOLLS' HOUSE MAGAZINE
OUTDOOR PHOTOGRAPHY
BLACK & WHITE PHOTOGRAPHY
MACHINE KNITTING NEWS
BUSINESSMATTERS

The above represents a full list of all titles
currently published or scheduled to be published.
All are available direct from the Publishers or through
bookshops, newsagents and specialist retailers.
To place an order, or to obtain a complete catalogue, contact:

GMC Publications,
166 High Street, Lewes, East Sussex
BN7 1XU United Kingdom
Tel: 01273 488005 Fax: 01273 478606
E-mail: pubs@thegmcgroup.com

Orders by credit card are accepted